This best-selling novel — winner of the ECPA Gold Medallion Award for excellence in fiction — recreates one of the most compelling and sensitive portions of the Gospel narrative. Savor the sights, sounds, flavors, and moods of biblical Palestine. Enter the minds and hearts of Martha, Mary, and Lazarus as their sorrow gives way to joy, their doubts give birth to faith, and their lives become forever entwined with their Messiah. And experience the poignant transformation of Martha, a struggling-to-believe disciple whose encounter with her Lord creates a love story all its own.

Joyce Landorf

I Came To Love You Late

SPIRE BOOKS

Fleming H. Revell
A Division of Baker Book House Co
Grand Rapids, Michigan 49516

A Spire Book
Copyright © 1977 by Joyce Landorf
Spire Books are published by Fleming H. Revell
a division of Baker Book House Company
P.O. Box 6287, Grand Rapids, MI 49516-6287
All rights reserved

ISBN: 0-8007-8411-1

Twelfth printing, June 1993

Printed in the United States of America

TO the Marthas
everywhere who were
"cumbered with much serving"
and who now move in freedom
and yet still serve.

My special thanks to

Brenda Arnold
Sheila Rapp
Richard Baltzell
and my family
who *gave* to this book.

*And the Word became man and lived
  for a time among us,
and we viewed His glory . . . .*
                              John 1:14

1

THOUGH she was tired and unusually disheveled, the tall, rather elegant young woman began her descent down the stone steps to the great main hall below.

Her hair, once neatly coiled and collected at the nape of her neck, had long since broken away and was now spilling over her forehead and untidily cascading down her neck.

Her flaxen-colored tunic and even the wide colorful girdle around her waist were soiled and soaked by the long night of dedicated working and insane rushing.

Shifting her armload of bloodied linens to catch up some straggling ends, she straightened her back and abruptly stopped in mid step. She had been halfway down the steps when, for the first time in two sunsets, she stopped and saw what was really there.

Still standing on the steps and holding her foul-smelling linens, Martha leaned back against the coolness of the stone wall and surveyed the large open hall below her.

All the massive bronze wall lamps, the lamps on stands, and even the tiny, exquisite hanging lamps were lit. Their blazing fires illuminated the room. The whitewashed walls and hanging tapestries were bathed with a delicate rose glow, and the atmosphere was thick with oil scents and hazy smoke.

The great hall was not encumbered by furniture. However, by anyone's standards, the three small couches grouped at one end, the slim-legged Grecian chair at the opposite end, the richly woven carpets, the intricately wrought lamp standards, and several low tables scattered here and there were most impressive to the average citizen of Bethany.

Tonight, and for the past fortnight, the room was not dominated by its furnishings, but by all the kind, caring, and even curious people who packed into the spacious room and spilled out into the courtyard.

From her place on the stairs, Martha could see the activity which came and went in small explosions of movement. She was fascinated by the fact that while the room was simply teeming with people, they all moved and breathed in a haunting sort of way. They clustered about in small groups, and for the most part, their talk was a low rumbling sound. Yet every once in a while, as it was right at that moment, they fell absolutely silent. They looked up and waited, as if her appearance on the stairs meant she would make an announcement or give them some new news.

To her it felt a little like she had lost all or part of her hearing, and she thought, *It's uncanny. So many people, and all is so quiet.*

Since there was no change and their expectant, upturned faces waited for her, Martha shook her head no, and they fell back to their small groups. The low murmuring began once more.

The villagers and even friends from Jerusalem had begun gathering two days ago when this crisis had emerged, and they had seemed to sense that this time it was different—perhaps, the last.

By one wall lamp she could see a cluster of old men. *Great patriarchs of the faith*, she smiled. And then she thought how dear it was of them to be there. They had been her father's friends, and they stood, together, in what looked like a special tribute to her dead father's memory. Martha's thoughts were interrupted because she found it suddenly difficult to swallow the lump of grief which always seemed to form when she thought of her father. She missed him even yet, but quickly she reminded herself it had been eighteen winters and eighteen summers since he had gone. So she said, "*Now* is what counts." Her speech didn't do much for her. When she recognized the dark robes and full white beard of Jacob Ben Nathan, that didn't help much either.

Aye, she thought, and a flood of memories engulfed her. *How he loved my father!* She remembered how old Jacob had laughed and argued with her father in a *most* Jewish way, and the recollection made her relax her shoulders just a bit in spite of the night. But the lump grew larger in her throat.

She knew everyone milling quietly around in the huge hall below her, because her little village of Bethany was large enough to be interesting, far enough away from the bustling city of Jerusalem to be restful, and yet was small enough to cover details such as names, new babies, and deaths. The homes themselves were scattered over the steep hills like small white jewels surrounded by the lush green velvet of cypress, pine, and palm trees.

Of Bethany's forty-nine houses, one dominated the main hill with its own special grandeur. *It is funny,* Martha mused, *no one calls this place the house of Josiah Ben Jochanan. It is always called ''Martha's House.''* She wondered what her father would have thought of that.

Tonight the great house was filled with at least one person from each of the neighboring houses. While most came out of love, Martha suspected a few came (as they always did) just to watch the goings and comings of Bethany's most affluent household.

Standing here and there beside the groups of men were the womenfolk of Bethany, their veils covering their bowed heads. A quick, general glance confirmed what she already suspected, and disappointment edged itself deeper into her frown. Her sister's beautiful face was *not* among the faces below, and Martha's own face tightened with the frustration.

In the next instant, she forgot about her sister, Mary, because she found Hannah, and the sight of her melted away some of the disappointment. Hannah was the widow who lived one house to the west. Martha, though she had never mentioned it to anyone, admired Hannah's abundant strength and silent courage. She had been able to pick out Hannah because her face was turned upward and wet with tears. The light from the nearest hanging lamp sparkled on her face and highlighted her aged beauty. Her mouth, as Martha knew it would be, was forming silent, prayerful words of supplication.

"Blessed art thou, dear Hannah," Martha sighed.

They were all there; her friends, neighbors, kinfolk, and ser vants, and that they were there because of her brother's time o dying made their presence very sweet. She was touched by th whole scene and typically she had no idea how to handle th rush of love rising urgently within her. She was always at a los when coping with her unseen emotions. She turned her attention once again to the movements of the crowd. "Yes, almos everyone seems to be here except for Mary," she sighed.

Weaving in and out of little knots of people, like the trim shuttles on a weaver's loom, were the servant girls. They worked their way through everyone, but even in their urgen rushing they were curiously still. Their bare feet flew noiselessly over the carpets, stone floors, and up and down the steps.

Martha spotted vivacious Deborah taking a small lamp to be refilled with oil, but she could see that the usual sparkle o Deborah's plain face was gone, and it was expressionless and pale. Martha saw Leah, another servant girl, and her face—in direct contrast to Deborah's—was beautiful, but set and solemn as if it had been hewn out of polished marble. The two girls passed each other without a word or a glance.

Martha silently murmured her thanks to them and marveled at their endurance and strength. Whether it was water jars balanc ing delicately on their heads, or clean linen held aloft in their hands, they seemed to move determinedly and effortlessly through the maze of people, steps, and corridors.

In spite of her weariness and the horror which was spending itself out in the room above her, Martha smiled when she saw Tabitha pass by Deborah and Leah as if they had been standing stone-still.

Tiny, amazing Tabitha, she said to herself. *Your name means "gazelle," and whoever named you called you rightly.* Tabitha did indeed move with the speed and grace of a young, healthy doe. In fact, she outran, outworked, and outscrubbed just about everyone, Martha recalled. The little mite of a girl passed Martha on the steps with no words but quick understanding glances.

There it was again—the low murmuring or the eerie quietness.

t was what had stopped her on her way in the first place. It was
all so strange. This huge, great hall was filled with people keeping their vigil during the night's deathwatch; yet everything was
happening with so little noise. Once in a while she could hear the
yipping of a hyena or jackal from the surrounding hills, but apart
from that and the occasional moaning from upstairs, the silence
fitted down over the great house like a shroud covering a corpse.

Martha trembled with an involuntary shiver, smoothed some
damp hair out of her eyes with her forearm, and realizing how
time had passed, she sternly took herself to task for being on the
stairs so long.

Where is Mary? again she questioned. *She should be up there
with him. Even if he is sleeping, he needs her presence. Where
has she been all night?* It was as if she had vanished with the first
night's wind.

Martha breathed in a breath of the hot, close air and resolved
firmly, as she knew she had to, to continue her tasks of the night,
with or without Mary. Briskly she moved down the steps. When
she reached the main floor, everyone wordlessly parted like the
Red Sea had done for Moses, and she moved straight and tall
through the midst of them. She was striding past their concerned, worried faces and would have reached the cooking area
without a word to anyone had it not been for the constraining
arm of Rabbi Ben Isaiah.

"How does it go up there with our Lazarus?" he whispered,
motioning with his head towards the stairs.

She became a little vexed with him for detaining her, because
she felt she'd already idled away far too much time. Besides, she
had left Lazarus alone because he was resting, so now she was
anxious to get back. However, she showed no impatience, because she was obliged to respect him and the sadness clinging to
his words was warm and genuine. Martha also knew the rabbi
was not there tonight to gossip outside the synagogue or down in
the town's small marketplace in the morning. He was there because he loved Lazarus.

In fact, she mumbled to herself with some resignation, *doesn't
everyone love my brother?*

Sickly and pale as he was, even from his childhood, Lazarus

had somehow managed to put everyone at ease about his obvi
ous illness, and in what seemed like only moments, he forge
lifelong friendships with family and friends alike. *That* she coul
never understand, but long ago she had accepted Lazarus's abil
ity to make instant friends as one of her brother's gifts. A gift sh
did not have.

"Now, Rabbi," she faced him directly and shifted her offen
sively sour clothes to her hip away from his face. "You know
our God has blessed Lazarus with many gifts. However, good
health has not exactly been one of them. My good brother has
been sick for all of his thirty years here in our house, and we
have seen him like this before. Please take heart. I'm just sure he
will come through even this."

Seeing that her words had not convinced him completely, she
spoke up, a trifle sharply, "You seem to be forgetting, dear
Rabbi, I am no novice in the techniques of healing." Hostility
like a small creature, ran through her statement, and the rabbi
caught it instantly.

He hastily tried to prove his loyalty to her and her father's
house by countering, "Oh, my dear child, I am not *un*aware of
your ministering virtues, Martha. Blessed you be. The whole of
Bethany knows and gratefully acknowledges your healing
hands." Then his voice faltered a bit, but he continued. "It's
just that this time . . . this time the crisis is so prolonged.
Lazarus took to his pallet last autumn. I remember it well be
cause it was right after the Feast of Tabernacles, and, dear
Martha, he is still there. In fact, his condition has worsened, and
well," he finished lamely, "you know it's almost spring, and
he's no better."

I don't need a reminder about my brother or the seasons! Her
thoughts bristled within her. She managed to quell the rising
rebellion inside her and gave the rabbi a tight smile. Respectfully
she said, "He *will* survive. You'll see." She hoped her words
had rung of experienced confidence, but the shaking of the old
rabbi's head told her she had not been very successful.

Cautiously he leaned closer. "I wish to make a suggestion *if* I
may."

Martha wondered if, in her whole lifetime, she had ever heard Rabbi Ben Isaiah *ask* for permission to make a suggestion. She was sure she hadn't.

"By all means, honored teacher," she said. *As if I could stop you,* she thought. For an instant a small smile played about her mouth.

"Your friend Jesus has healed so many. I was wondering if you had considered asking for his intervention." He finished with his hands piously folded together near the top of his chest.

Martha almost laughed out loud. There stood her dear, old, trusted rabbi suggesting she call Jesus, while he himself had publicly and privately said, "I am one rabbi who will have to have the carpenter's claims *proven* beyond any doubt before I believe he is who he says he is."

"Why, Rabbi Ben Isaiah, are you changing your mind about the man who walks among us humbly, speaking as no other ruler, leader, or prophet has ever done?" she gently chided.

He tugged at his beard. *That Martha is as smart as three quick men all rolled together,* his thoughts pronounced. "I only meant he is your friend, and his reputation for healing grows larger each day. I would have thought you would have asked him to heal Lazarus long before this."

Now she was getting annoyed, and with the smallest speck of respect in her tone, she said, "Rabbi, it is *precisely* because he *is* our friend that we have never taken advantage of him in Lazarus's behalf. We have enjoyed him in our home, but Lazarus himself has always cautioned us against petitioning him. Now, forgive me, but I have spent far too long away from my duties."

The rabbi, understanding more about people than she did in those moments, pretended not to notice her tone of voice, but it was an awkward time for both of them. Martha knew her tongue was too outspoken, especially for a woman, but she was wearily past the point of carefully choosing her words.

She was grateful for the sputtering of a lamp behind him, and with one quick gesture she signaled passing Deborah to replenish the oil. The girl caught the look and nodded affirmatively.

As Martha bolted from the great hall, the rabbi tugged on his beard and muttered, "That one never misses a thing."

Martha constantly nettled the rabbi with her efficiency, her planning, and her tongue, which could be sharper than a double-edged sword, but he had to admire her good heart and the way she got things done. *My, how proud Josiah would have been of his Martha tonight,* he chuckled and amended his thinking to include Lazarus and Mary. *All of them are fine children, and they would make any father's heart beat with pride,* he mused as he watched her go.

He had often observed and compared Martha's plain features to Mary's beauty, but he had to admit that while Mary was startlingly beautiful with her flame red hair and luminous blue eyes, it was Martha who adjusted to any situation in exactly the proper way. *Yes,* he repeated to himself, *Josiah would be proud.*

Breaking away from the rabbi and the others, Martha finally reached the large cooking area. She was almost swallowed into a sea of frenzied activity. The room with its whitewashed walls, its hanging lamps, cupboards, tables, and baskets of lentils and beans was bursting with human bodies. Everyone was working on their appointed tasks: bringing in the filled water pots, taking soiled linen outside to be washed, or merely standing alert for her directions.

Without counting, Martha knew for certain that no servant or slave was in his bed taking his ease. They were all there, present and accounted for. They, too, loved Master Lazarus. Their obvious show of love made her frustration with Mary's absences grow larger.

They must all know he's dying, she thought. Because she knew it too, the hard knot which had lain heavily in her abdomen for weeks slowly, but surely, burned with a searing, unbearable heat. Martha knew her face must have registered her pain when Naomi, laying her leathery, spotted hand on her arm, asked, "Are you ailing, too?"

"No, I am not ill, and you must not worry, Naomi. In fact, you should be on your pallet, for you will need your rest come the dawn."

The old woman did not leave but sat down on the nearest low

tool. "I cannot sleep," she said simply. Her tears began to flow down her face. The creases and lines made tiny riverbeds for the tears, and she made no attempt to stop the flow or dry up the source.

"Will Lazarus . . . ?"

Unable to pronounce the word *die,* she broke off, leaning her head against the wall. The flow of tears turned the unchecked streams into rivers of salty water, and she was powerless to stop it. Grimly she waited for Martha's answer.

Naomi was not only the oldest woman servant of the household, but the dearest and most highly respected as well. It was Martha who oversaw each detail that transpired in the household. She had taken over the responsibility years ago, but Naomi had been there first.

Martha, still holding her linens, squatted down beside the white-haired woman and recalled how dear old Naomi had lovingly taken care of all of them when they were little. She had been, in effect, a second mother even though no blood ties connected them.

Josiah Ben Jochanan and his lovely Galilean wife, Rachel, had rejoiced thirty-two years ago at the birth of their firstborn—a strong, husky, and surprisingly large baby girl. Jointly they agreed to name her Martha. It was an appropriate and even prophetic name for it means "lady" or "mistress of the house."

Two years later the same loving union gave them a son. That he was small and exceedingly frail was of no consequence to them, because he was the product of their love.

Three years passed, and their third child was born. She was a tiny girl, who was as fair in skin coloring, with flaming red hair, as Martha was ivory skinned and dark raven haired. But with her birth came the first real sadness for the family of Josiah Ben Jochanan.

Only moments after Rachel had glimpsed the bright, exquisite face of her newest daughter, she died in Josiah's arms with Naomi clutching the tiny babe.

Later Josiah, remembering a loving conversation whispered weeks before her death, named the infant Mary, as Rachel had wished.

The day of Mary's birth, Naomi had inherited instant mother hood to two children and one baby. She had done her job wit loving devotion, and even after her fingers lost their quickness and were bent and rigid, she continued to live there and to lov each of them.

However, Martha had suspected, with no rancor whatsoeve that it had always been Lazarus who had captured most strongl the old woman's heart.

Suddenly, the stench from the linen jolted Martha back int the night, and quickly she dropped the mess into a large empt basket.

Still down on her knees beside Naomi's stool, Martha crispl said, "Naomi, look at me." Martha had the vexing ability t speak, command, and delegate authority much like a Roma centurion. It was quite noticeable that when she spoke, mos people tended to look and listen. So it was at that momen However, Naomi kept her hands clamped over her mouth a though she was afraid a cry might escape and shatter the dee stillness in the house. Without taking her hands away, she duti fully looked into Martha's deep, brown eyes.

"Are you listening?" Martha's tone was gentle, but intense She waited for the woman's nod and then continued. "Now, here she evenly measured out her words. "I want you to re member how many times in the past year you have seen thi fiery fever and weakness come upon Lazarus and take its toll o him. Remember, too, that between God, you, and me, we hav *always* brought him back. Is this not so?"

Naomi dropped her hands from her face and lifted the corne of her skirt to dry her face. She wiped her cheeks and slowl nodded her head in agreement. For just a second there was glimmer of relief on her face, but it vanished quickly as sh blurted out, "But, Mistress Martha, never have these old eye beheld his sickness so strong or for so long. This time the fire i his body and the issue of blood that streams from him is mor . . . more than ever in the past."

Ignoring the truth of Naomi's statement, Martha stubbornly went on. "Believe me, it will be as before. You'll see. We wil bring him through. We shall."

"But it is all so *different* this time," Naomi wailed. Then, as if she had a sudden inspirational solution, she touched Martha's shoulder and whispered, "Will you send for *him?*"

Martha pretended ignorance to gain time and asked, "Who?"

Sharply Naomi breathed aloud, "My dear Martha, you *know* who I mean."

Wearily, Martha uttered, "I'm sorry, Naomi. I don't have time to go into this with you, but, no, I am not going to send word to Jesus." She stood up now, tall and authoritative before the old woman.

Naomi looked up and pleaded, "But he loves you and all of this household. Has he not called this place his 'house of renewal'? If he knew of Lazarus's terrible state, he would willingly come." Then, to reinforce her own thoughts, she added brightly, "And once here, he would make everything alright."

Martha's voice, heavy with extreme fatigue and edged with anger, said a determined, "No."

"But," Naomi implored.

"No!" And this time it was thundered rather than spoken. As soon as she had said it, Martha was sorry for her outburst. She bent over, put her hand on Naomi's shoulder, apologized, and said, "It's just that Jesus has troubles of his own. Why should he take on ours, too?" Naomi was barely listening, but Martha continued. "He has told us and all his men that he will be rejected and shunned by the elect of the priesthood, elders, and scribes alike. The last time we saw Peter, he told us Jesus had even predicted his own death. I did not really believe that he would go that far, but then only a few days ago I was told by Uncle Tobias that Jesus narrowly escaped being stoned to death in the city. Can you see, Naomi? I cannot ask him to come when his own circumstances are so dangerously fragile."

Martha was too tired to go into all the frightening rumors she had heard. She wondered if, even for Lazarus, she had the right to ask Jesus to risk his life in coming to Bethany. She would have said more, but she was embarrassed by the awareness that everyone in the cooking area was intently listening. All were soaking up her words like sponges.

The sight of them was like a finger snapping loudly in her

head, forcing her back into reality, and quickly she jumped up
springing into immediate action like an arrow shot from a strong
bow.

"You, Joseph," she directed. "I have run out of clean wet
cloths for his fever. See if any are ready yet from the washing
trough." Then, turning, she said, "Leah, go with him and bring
as many as you can. Tabitha, I have not seen my sister since
dark. Please find her and tell her to come upstairs. Be your usual
quick self." Her tone softened, and she was about to continue
setting everything in a more orderly way when the hushed night
air was slashed in two by a long, piercing scream. Everyone
became a solid statue, as if they were made of stone, and held
their positions.

The scream was still ripping through the night when Martha
gathering her thick, long skirts in one hand and pushing
everyone out of the way with the other, bounded out past hor
rified people in the main room. She took the steps two at a time
to the chamber upstairs. She could hear the clamoring question
of the people below, and it sounded like a lion roaring in the
distance.

Naomi, finding speed from some bygone year of her youth
followed closely behind in a frantic scramble, and both women
came to an abrupt halt in the doorway of Lazarus's room.

The young girl just inside the doorway, with the broken water
vessel at her feet, was still screaming. In one quick gesture
Martha clamped her hand over the girl's mouth and hissed
"Deborah, stop it! That's enough!" Promptly it silenced her, but
the terror was still in the girl's large, wide-open, brown eyes
For a moment Martha matched Deborah's stare with a meaning
ful glare, and when she had the situation under control, she took
her hand away and turned to focus on the horror which had
evoked the girl's hysteria.

Blood was everywhere. Martha had never seen so much
Even when she had brought forth the most complicated birthing
of babies as a midwife, she had not seen such a flow of blood
Naomi clutched the doorpost and endlessly sobbed, "My God
my God."

Martha picked her way through the broken pottery, her san

dals slipping in the mixture of spilled water and discharged blood, and slowly, like in a bad dream, she made her way over to his pallet.

The thick hem of her dress soaked up the grim liquid and got heavy with it before she reached him. Her pace towards him seemed to take forever.

Where is all this coming from? she puzzled. *How could one emaciated, sick man spill out so much of life and so quickly?* Her thoughts raced a hundred times faster than her feet.

She had not been gone that long, she reasoned to herself. It was only a few minutes. She remembered when she had left him, his cheeks had been flushed and reddened and he had been burning to touch, but when she had asked how he felt, he had answered with a slight affirmative nod of his head. He had even managed a flicker of a smile. Thus she had left him unattended, not pleased with progress, but satisfied with circumstances. Now this! She despaired as she looked down on his death white face.

He breathed a few short gasps as she watched, then lay still, only to startle her a second later with more quick intakes of air. With each movement of his chest, she expected the end. But after a few minutes of watching, she recalled some of the dying people she had seen, who breathed in this strange way for days (once even for a week) before dying.

"Naomi!" she called. "This is not the time for sobbing but for scrubbing. Help me clean him up and set this room in order."

Naomi stopped her moaning and stammered, "But, isn't he dead?"

"No." Martha made her way over to the doorway and impatiently said, "He has no reason to be alive, but he is. As long as there is a flicker of life in his body, I shall see to his needs. Now, *move!*"

For the better part of two hours they all washed, soaked up the mess, and stole anxious glances at the pale shell of a man. Finally everything was as before except, of course, for Lazarus. He was on the knife-edge of his life, and when Martha looked on him, she began to prepare herself for his death morning.

She had dearly paid for her mistake of leaving him unattended;

so she began to prepare to stay by his side until it was over. However, both Naomi and Leah asked if they could watch him and relieve her for a few hours. Martha, fatigued beyond belief and touched by their caring love, wearily agreed and left the two of them beside his pallet.

Disheartened and tired, she came down the stairs and told the still-waiting friends that Lazarus seemed to be resting and they should go to their homes. She promised to send immediate word should his condition change. Reluctantly, they began to leave, but two old women and one man refused to abandon their deathwatch. She tried reasoning with them, but her tongue was thick with fatigue, and she lost her ability to give sense to her words. In the end, she let them stay. Martha tended the lamps, put out the fires in the big ones, and left several small ones burning, and murmured her good night to the solemn figure sitting in the hall. She then checked the cooking area and back entrances to be sure that every one of the household had gone to his pallet.

Exhausted of spirit and wearied beyond physical endurance, she forced herself up the inner staircase once more.

Once she reached the upper floor, she merely put her head inside the doorway and watched his uneven breathing sequence until she was satisfied there had been no change. She looked at the women, nodded, and gestured toward the roof. They understood and settled down to their vigil.

When she left them, she moved to an outside doorway and eventually wound her way up on an outside staircase to the upper roof.

How long have I been down there? she wondered, and then she remembered, only two days and two nights. But somehow this had been so different. The room below her had been stifling hot and rancid with the smell of dying. *It is good to be up here,* she thought as she reached the top step of the narrow stairway which led to the roof.

But never had she been so drained.

2

WHEN she stepped out on to the roof, the moon was full, and everything was bathed and shimmering in its delicate, silvery light.

Bethany's night wind, which always kissed the earth and the whitewashed houses with its coolness each evening, was gently perfuming the air with various fragrances.

The majestic scent of cedar, cypress, and pine trees was sprinkled with the soft, light aroma of spring flowers which had just burst into splashes of color in the gardens below and the hills beyond.

The only sounds up there now were the songs of the crickets and other small creatures who were performing their simple musical patterns out in their hillside amphitheater.

Bordering the large roof on three sides were low stout walls, whitewashed and gleaming in the moon's illumination. The long back side of the roof supported a narrow third-level room. Martha used it for storing extra supplies and foodstuffs, but sometimes, when they had a houseful of guests in the height of the summer's heat and dryness, she cleaned it out and used it for cool sleeping quarters.

At one end attached to the front of this room was a large fringed canopy. It was held out from the walls by three sturdy wooden poles. During the day its shade provided a lonely respite from the sun's searing rays, but at night it provided a dark, rather private place for contemplation.

Scattered over the rooftop itself were large, flat, woven drying trays and wide baskets. Because it was spring, the trays were empty now, but they were stained and fragrant with the juice from the last harvest of figs, grapes, and apricots. Here and there, in the midst of the baskets and trays, stood some gracefully designed pottery storage jars. Up on the wall, Martha had started small fruit trees by planting them in little wooden tubs. They stood like miniature sentries around the wall and gently bent with the breeze.

The moon's light was so bright that the darkest place on the roof was the area under the canvas canopy, but all of it escaped Martha. None of the night's sounds, sights, or even the roof's lone occupant was seen by the fatigued woman.

Almost as if she were in a trance, Martha moved across the expansive roof, picked her way around some large jars, and crumpled down on the edge of the roof wall just in front of the canopied area.

Her feelings were unreal as if they did not belong to her but floated out around her. Her body was there, but she couldn't feel anything. Her eyes were open, but she saw nothing. She spoke and was unaware that her words were being heard. "I feel like a wilted tamarisk blossom," she sighed. She couldn't remember being so tired. *Even my bones are tired,* she realized. The skin over her cheekbones seemed stretched to its limit, and her head was persistently pounding with pain. She was gray with fatigue, but she resolved anew that she would not give in. "I'll hold out," she said aloud, but she wasn't sure *how.*

Suddenly she blurted out, "My God, have You abandoned me? Lazarus is dying. I've done all I could do. No, I've done more than anyone. Will You snatch him away, too?" Her thoughts became jagged, rough spoken utterances. Had she been given to cursing (as the widow woman who lived in the small cave on the lower hillside), she would have screamed her obscenities to the whole of Bethany. *Yes,* she thought, *even to the smallest star on the edge of the darkest part of the night.* However, she couldn't ignore the coolness of the night on the roof, and it soothed her, but her thoughts continued to pour out of her as if her soul were a broken vessel.

"Like a thief in the night, You have stolen my mother, father, even my bridegroom. And now, again in the night, are You stealing my brother, too?"

Some of what she said and felt got through to her, because she found herself a bit shocked at what she had voiced. Never, ever, had she vocalized her frustrations about God's will to anyone, much less to God! Yet the words continued to drain out of her heart.

"I do not begin to see the wisdom of all this. He suffers wordlessly; yet he continues to suffer. His pain is more than I can bear; yet the thought of his dying runs a dagger through me. Dear God, I have seen so much of sickness and death. Must I see even more?"

For once Martha let her hot, stinging tears stream down her face. The rigidness seemed to melt out of her neck and spine, and as the tears were released, she bent over and laid her head in her arms on her knees. Her sobbing stabbed the night with sound.

She did not know how long she sat like that or whether it was the cry or the cool wind which refreshed her, but slowly she felt a little better. She eased herself down off the wall and sat on the rooftop itself. An early spring rain had patted down the earth, and the cool, moist air seemed to slow her breathing and anger.

Leaning with her back braced by the wall, she said aloud of past memories, "You know, my Lord, I don't ever remember being alive without the sword of death hanging over my head."

She recalled her mother's death and remembered that her father's sobbing could be heard in the farthest corner of their majestic stone house.

Lazarus, only three years old at the time, knew only by his father's wailing that something was terribly wrong. He stayed on his pallet with Naomi bending over him, doing her best to calm his fears.

Martha, at five, knew better. She was already a serious child by nature, and her mother's death made her even more somber.

Their neighbor Hannah had discovered Martha standing stoically in the hall outside Rachel's room. She had picked the little girl up, held her on her broad lap, and sang soft little songs to her. But it was to no avail. Martha's young mind sensed that because of the night's events, everything would be changed.

The morning after her mother died, Martha solemnly watched

as the women bathed and prepared the body for burial in the family sepulcher. Had they seen her, she would not have been allowed to stay. But she was so small and still, and the women so preoccupied, that no one caught sight of her.

Some would say later of the day that it was the moment when a five-year-old girl grew into womanhood. It was true. For Martha seemed, from that day forward, to accept death and dying, and in small ways she began to carry out a few adult responsibilities. Overnight she became the self-appointed guardian and mother to both her brother and infant sister, almost totally ignoring Naomi's mothering efforts.

She interrupted her recollections by voicing out loud, "Yes, all this time I've taken my mother's place and for the last eighteen years *even* my father's position."

"Mother," she said absently to the night winds. "Mother, you would be proud of me, I think, for I have tried to do my very best."

Deliberately, to change her thoughts and depressing mood, she began to concentrate on identifying the night's fragrances. She started with the tiny, white, star-shaped blossoms on one of her fledgling orange trees and worked through a couple of others. She even caught the faint whiff of roasting lamb. It roused her sense of taste and reminded her of how long it had been since she had eaten.

Who, in all of Bethany, would be cooking this time of night? she idly wondered. *Who, but thoughtful Hannah,* she realized. *No wonder Hannah left early tonight. She wanted to provide for us tomorrow. How dear of her.*

The pain in her head was still persistent, but now it had enlarged and moved down into her neck and shoulder muscles. It was demanding her full attention. She massaged around her neck and spent some time trying to loosen the hard ropes which seemed to be strangling her, but it was of no use. Everything was knotted into pain. Her mind went back to Lazarus.

How many times have I done this for him? She smiled in a rueful manner as she remembered how one of the villagers, a vulgar man, had teased her about her ability to rub and massage away pain. He had coarsely suggested she go to Jerusalem and open up a massage shop next to the Romans' public bathhouse.

All her life she had been good with her healing hands, and she knew it with confidence, not conceit; yet she could not tolerate her failure with Lazarus.

It was all so puzzling to her. She was Bethany's mainstay for the sick. If a woman ailed or a baby was born, if a man was dying or if someone had been injured in an accident, they always sent for her. The villagers knew they could depend on Martha's calmness, her gift with herbs and ointments, and her talented healing hands.

For months now she had used on Lazarus every magical brew of herbs she had ever known. She had wrapped him in every poultice imaginable, and she had done everything there was to do.

But now the overwhelming fatigue had robbed her of the ability to think clearly, and as a sudden squally storm could stir a calm lake into a frenzy, she became more depressed and blurted out, "Why, then, have I failed so much? I've lost my precious family. I was unable to save any of them. Am I to lose Lazarus, too? Am I to fail again?"

Out of the dark area under the canopy a voice quietly answered.

"We could send for the Master."

Martha heard the voice, and the words hit her with the force of a lightning bolt in a thunderstorm. She was up on her feet instantly. On her ascent up, her arm hit two basket trays and sent them flying over the wall and thudding about on the ground below.

Immediately Martha remembered how she had sought for Mary earlier and how Mary had simply vanished into the night. Without warning Martha's anger boiled to the surface of her mind and tongue. She stood in the middle of the roof in front of the canopy, both hands on her hips, and spit out a torrential flow of words, accusations, and penetrating questions.

"Mary! Where have you been all night? I needed you. Why didn't you come and help me? I sent Tabitha to find you. Don't you know Lazarus almost died?" She was on the edge of screaming now. "Why did you stay away?" Finally, she shouted the three vital words which were burning within her. *"Where were you?"*

Mary came out from the awning's darkness and stood directly in front of Martha. Her hair was all covered by a veil, but her face shone in the moonlight because of the wetness of her cheeks. She was shaking, not because of the night's chill, but because she'd never seen or heard Martha so angry.

At first she just stood there, with no words to explain her absence. Finally, in her soft but clear, warm voice, Mary slowly confessed, "I've been up here, my sister." She put her head down. "I could not come to you. You know how any sickness of others produces my own inner illness. I would have been no good to you in his room. Besides, it was better that I stay here and pray." She looked up and searched Martha's face for understanding.

"Pray?" snapped Martha. "Pray—when all of Bethany was in our house? When I have so much to worry about, you disappear and make an added worry? When everyone had so many tasks to tend? When our brother would have been soothed by your presence? You stayed up here and *prayed?"*

Her exasperation with Mary knew no limits! After a moment's pause, she continued her tirade, only now her voice was dripping with sarcasm.

"Well, Mary, my dear sister, when you were up here praying, did God answer your prayers or shed any wisdom on our circumstances?"

Mary, sensitive to the events which provoked Martha's rage, ignored the tone of her sister's question and answered evenly, "Yes, Martha, He did answer. He is a loving God and full of justice and mercy."

Abruptly Martha turned, leaving her sister, and walked to the roof's edge to absently look down the main hill road which led towards Jerusalem.

Mary moved behind her, and after hesitating for a moment, she took ahold of Martha's arm and said carefully, "I think it is God's will that we send for Jesus. He loves our brother. They are the dearest of friends. We have never asked the Master for healing. But now we need him if Lazarus is to be restored." She did not catch Martha's impatient sigh.

Grateful for the passing of a sudden gust of cold wind, Martha used the difficult moment to pick up an old shawl which had been left on the edge of a jar. After she pulled the shawl around her shoulders, she clearly, and surprisingly without hostility, said, "If he really is who he says he is—God," she pronounced the name skeptically, "then we would not *have* to send for him. He would already *know* we needed him."

Mary's skin prickled at the back of her neck ever so slightly as she heard her sister's nearly blasphemous statement.

Martha waited for her words to sink in and then, looking directly at Mary, said, "Don't condemn me with those righteous eyes of yours, my sister. You know you have already wondered why Jesus has not come on his own before this, haven't you?"

Mary knew full well she was no match for Martha's logical debates; so she simply shrugged her shoulders and answered, "Honestly, I know somewhere in your words are buried truths, but it would take wisdom beyond my understanding and logic beyond my ability to unravel the mysteries of what you have just said."

Lamely at first, and then tenderly but with more authority, she went on. "All I know is that tonight as I prayed, I felt we should send for the Master. From there, my sister, I just don't know."

Mary's openness had more than once softened Martha, and tonight her humble attitude plus her genuine loving honesty flowed over Martha like a warm, fragrant oil, soothing away the exhausted woman's feelings.

It is such a bewildering, confusing time, Martha thought. *One moment I am angry and shouting, and the very next moment I am sad and inwardly weeping. All the order seems to have gone out of my life, and now I have lashed out at Mary; yet she answers me with soft truthfulness and gentle love.*

Martha turned, shook her head, and with glistening eyes, embraced her sister. "I am truly sorry I spoke so harshly, beloved one," Martha apologized, patting her sister's shoulders. "Forgive me. My mind does not seem to be pulling together as it always has." Inside she felt as if her life was a cart hitched up to two unequally yoked animals, with a horse pulling one way and an ox pulling the other. Everything was so wrong and so baffling. She longed for the clear, decisive world of a few days ago.

Mary pulled away and studied Martha in a peculiar, searching way. It was obvious that some unseen thought had unbelievably formed itself into a startling realization, and looking directly at Martha, she said, "But you still don't think we should send for Jesus, do you, Martha?"

Martha tried to sound nonchalant. "No. It is simply that I am not sure we have the right to ask." She then brought up the friendship of the past three years and how it would be an imposition for Jesus to come. She continued, over Mary's softly voiced objections, with the fact that Jesus was in precarious circumstances as it was.

She would have gone on with her list of arguments except that Mary cut to the heart of it with, "You think it's too late for Lazarus! That's it, isn't it? You think he'll be dead before we can reach the Master. You don't think Jesus will reach here in time, is that it?"

Martha gave in and affirmatively nodded her head. Mary had the uncanny ability to sense the core of a problem and dig up the deep, covered-up issues of the heart. On this one, she had hit Martha dead center with her arrow of truth.

Mary touched Martha's cheek and turned her face toward her own and directly questioned, "He is that sick? Lazarus is really so sick that he may die in a few days?" Her voice was breaking here and there.

Martha turned away and said flatly, "No. He may be already dead. He spilled much of his lifeblood tonight, and his body was burning with more heat than I've ever seen or felt before. His breathing comes in jerks and pauses like the steps of an old man coming down a dangerous, steep path. One does not know when the next breath will come, or if it will come at all. He lies with a death mask on his face."

"Oh, don't," Mary cried. "Don't say those things."

"I'm sorry, dear sister, but it is true." Martha straightened up, tall and unbending, and matter-of-factly smoothed her hair so it was all caught under the coiled braid at the nape of her neck. After adjusting her shawl, she said, "Come, we will go to ιim. I will show you what I mean.''

Mary did not move or respond.

"Mary, Mary," Martha walked up behind her and said softly
n her ear. "Dear sister, I know Jesus *can* heal. Haven't we both
seen him with our own eyes?''

Mary nodded.

"It's just that this time," Martha hesitated. "This time, it's
oo late. Lazarus has been sick too long, and time has run out for
ιim.''

"Then you are forgetting our kinsfolk in Capernaum." Mary's
quiet voice chilled the air.

"Our kinsfolk?" Martha wondered aloud. "Oh, yes," she
said as she remembered. "You mean our mother's brother and
ιis account of Sarah's recovery.''

"Sarah's recovery?" Mary stared at her sister. "It was much
more than a recovery! Uncle Jairus said she had *died;* yet Jesus
raised her from the deep pool of death and brought her back!''

"But," Martha stammered, "that was different.''

"Different, how?" demanded Mary.

"Well," Martha's tone was getting impatient, "Sarah never
had been sick a day in all of her brief twelve years. She could
have merely had a sleeping sickness which overcame her that
morning and then . . . .''

"No!" Mary's voice was strained and taut. "That's not what
happened. She was dead, not sleeping, and Jesus raised her.
Besides, Philip and Andrew both told us about being with Jesus
in the city of Nain and how a widow's son was raised from the
dead . . . .''

"All this talk is needless," Martha broke in. "Think of all the
stories we have heard of Jesus, Mary. How could one person do
so many things and be in so many places? Besides, I tell you, it is
different for our Lazarus.''

"I know what's the matter with you, Martha." Mary was as
close to raising her voice as she had ever been. "You believe
Jesus can do *certain* things, like healing people, but only up to a
point or under the right circumstances. You think of Jesus as
another Simeon, the magician—a person who can do *some*
magic tricks, but not all. You've turned our Master into a magi-

cian, and a limited magician at that!" Her subdued fury flun
itself noisily into the night.

"That's not true!" Martha angrily countered, as she grippe
Mary's shoulders. "I *believe* in his divine gifts . . . I've see
him heal . . . I know his power. It's just that I have also see
Lazarus." Then, gesturing towards the sky with her hand, sh
continued. "While you've been up here 'communing' with God
I've been watching our brother's life ebb away. He's almos
gone. If Jesus were here now—this moment—I believe he coul
put the light back into Lazarus's eyes. But he's not here, and
just know it's too late. I have to be realistic about this. I also
know there is a time to be born and a time to die, and from
everything I've seen, it is Lazarus's time."

Seeing she was getting nowhere, Martha abruptly took charge
and guided her sister across the roof to the stairway, tersely
saying, "Come, see for yourself."

The moon was slipping down behind one set of hills, and the
sun was creeping up over the other. The crickets had slowed
their song almost to a complete stop as the two young women
made their way down the outside staircase.

They entered Lazarus's large chamber to discover that Naom
and Leah had fallen into an exhausted sleep. While everything
appeared to be pretty much as it had been, Martha instantly
knew something was different. She hurried to him.

His dark brown hair and beard were damp to her touch as she
smoothed it. His eyes opened, and though deep, dark half-
circles lay under them, Martha thought she saw a glimmer of his
old sparkle, and suddenly she was encouraged.

"Martha," Lazarus said faintly, and she leaned closer to
catch each word. "Is it morning yet?" The sleeping women
awoke with a start at the sound of his voice.

*What a delight! What wonderment! Not only did he recognize
her, but he asked a reasonable question. Was he better?*
Martha's thoughts raced wildly. Behind her, Mary questioned,
"What did he say?"

Smiling, Lazarus said, "If someone would draw back the
tapestries, I could tell if it is morning, if only *someone* would
. . . ." He spoke quite clearly, and everyone heard.

Thank heaven, even his sense of humor is alive! Martha's thoughts flashed, and she breathed deeply. Naomi and Leah left hurriedly to tell the others of this miraculous change.

"Mary, pull back the curtains." Martha's command was almost joyous.

Lazarus's room faced the east, and since the first rosy haze of dawn had begun, the light filtered in—pale, but lovely.

Is it the warm color of the morning sun, or is it really his coloring that tells me he looks better? Is he, or is the sun playing tricks on me? Martha wondered. He did look so much better. She was still unable to take it all in. But just as she was sorting it all out in her mind, Mary tugged at her arm and silently motioned her to follow.

Out in the hall, using guarded, whispered tones, both women began talking at once.

"It's a sign!" Mary enthused.

"Maybe Jesus has already healed him!" Martha hopefully theorized.

"That may be true, but shouldn't we send for Jesus, anyway?" Mary urged.

"Yes, perhaps that's wise." Martha surprised herself with her abrupt turnabout.

Together they went back to him.

"What are you two planning?" Lazarus asked and managed a weak smile.

"We thought you'd like to see the Master," Mary explained.

He nodded and ever so softly said, "Yes, yes. I'd like that. I am lonely to see his face, and it would be good to hear his voice."

On hearing this, Martha left them hurriedly, and her words "I'll see to it" made them smile knowingly at each other.

Mary was on familiar ground with this Lazarus, and she could freely give of herself to his needs. It was the other Lazarus, the one impaled by the sword of pain or quivering on the brink of death, to whom she was of no help at all. Only Martha could treat and minister on those days. But this morning, with him so improved, she was pleased that Martha had left her in charge of him, and she was filled with a contagious kind of joy.

Mary perched herself on the edge of his pallet like a small sparrow on a tree branch, and for some time they needed no words. They drank in the stillness and the peace of the lovely dawn.

A bit later Mary questioned, "Could you sip some water, dear Lazarus?" He answered with something, but she missed it; so he spoke up and said, "No, nothing. Just sing for me."

Her laugh bubbled out of her, and she said, "Oh, no. I would sound like a frog croaking in the creek bed. Besides, what would I sing?"

He spoke slowly, but softly; so she bent closer to him to catch his words.

"When we were children, you made up songs for any occasion. Do it now," he whispered.

Delighted that he seemed so much better, Mary agreed and pulled a large cushion from his pallet, placed it on the floor nearest his head, and plopped down on it with childlike grace.

"Alright, big brother, but it might not be very good, and remember you'll have to add a verse of your own."

Her humming began immediately and so did the mischievous twinkle in her eyes. Lazarus silently watched the face of his beautiful sister, and she, catching the look of dear love, became even more beautiful.

After she thought and hummed a bit, she checked with him and asked playfully, "Are you ready for this?" He nodded and blinked one eyelid to show his approval.

The foolish little song, written in a moment and inspired by the moment, came liltingly out of Mary's clear and bell-like voice.

> Jesus is coming today, today.
> Oh, give him sparrows' wings on his feet,
> So he can fly to us, this day,
> This day.
>
> Jesus is coming today, today.
> Oh, give him foxes' feet,
> So he can run to us, this day,
> This day.

Here Lazarus chuckled softly. "You're right," he said. "It's
ot very good."
Ignoring him, with a look of mock indignation, she continued.

> Jesus is coming today, today.
> Oh, give him fast little rabbits' feet,
> So he can hop to us this day,
> This day.

Mary stopped her singing, and suppressing a small giggle, she
aid as sternly as she could, "Now, Lazarus, for the next verse
's your turn." Turning up her pert little nose, she said, "You'll
e how it takes a lot of natural talent to compose songs." She
ole a peek at him. He was still smiling.

"Come, now, it's your turn, Lazarus . . . Lazarus? . . ."
he touched his arm. The smile was there, but he was not.

Abruptly the song and the game were over. He had gone with-
ut a good-bye.

Still holding his arm, Mary was unable to move. The only
ound from her was her repeated cry of "Martha . . . Martha
. . Martha," but it was barely whispered; so no one heard, and
o one came.

3

When she had seen Lazarus's good color and heard his wea
but clear words, Martha bounded down the stairs with a nev
found supply of energy, rushed through the main floor of th
house into the cooking area, and almost knocked Naomi off h
feet.

"He's better, isn't he?" the old woman smiled as she asked

Martha flew past her and out the back entrance, into the sma
courtyard, and over to the men's sleeping quarters. While ru
ning, she shouted back over her shoulder, "Yes, *much* bette
You'll be happy to know, old dear, I am sending Joseph to fetc
Jesus." Naomi clasped her hands together and blessed the Lor
for answering her prayers.

It was not seemly that she go inside the men's quarters; s
Martha urgently knocked, opened the door, barely stuck he
head inside, and softly called, "Joseph?"

Samuel, Joseph's father, had tended the sheep and goat herd:
and as Joseph grew into manhood, his father taught him th
skills of shepherding.

Joseph was four years older than Martha and had never mar
ried. After the death of his father and Master Josiah, Marth
made Joseph the head overseer for the flocks and fields. H
served the Josiah Ben Jochanan family well, and Martha paid hi
wages affectionately, generously, and as if he were kinfolk.

When he thought he heard her voice in the yard, he appeare
almost at once while pulling on his outer tunic.

Joseph's first anxious questions were of Lazarus. Hurriedl
Martha told him of Lazarus's new turn for the better. As she wa
explaining her request that he find Jesus, someone tugged on he
sleeve.

"Mistress Martha?"

She turned to look down into the young, alert face of Aaron.

"What is it, my boy?" she asked impatiently.

"If it is runners you want to go get Jesus, we would like to go."

The pride and confidence ringing in hi. voice was rare in such a young servant, and Martha marveled at it.

"Who is 'we'?" she questioned.

"Oh, Jude and I," and he straightened his shoulders as he said it.

"Jude and Aaron. I might have known," Martha said with a grin playing around the corners of her mouth.

Both Aaron and Jude, now about ten years old, had been orphaned earlier, and though they were not related, you could hardly have one without the other.

Naomi had timidly brought the thin, spindle-legged Jude into the household. Mary had made a promise to a dying young mother on the outskirts of Bethany one day, and Aaron had solemnly clung to her hand as she brought him home.

For five years now the boys had lived in the servants' quarters, and in the midst of accomplishing Martha's small tasks, eating Naomi's good food, and developing under Joseph's fatherly hand, the boys flourished and became brothers.

"We talked yesterday," Aaron said earnestly, "and we hoped that if you wanted to send for the Master, you would let us go." As if to ensure his argument, he added, "We would be faster than Claudius's horse!"

Martha thought his choice of man and horse was excellent. She had always felt Claudius was very different from any Roman soldier she had ever known. He was a centurion who, unlike others, seemed to have a God-fearing soul and no one, she knew, had a horse like his. It was powerful and magnificent, since it was bred from Libyan stock. Claudius was frequently approached by a buyer eager to purchase the horse, but more often he was offered money for bets to race him.

Martha could not remember exactly when she had first met Claudius, but usually when Jesus was visiting them, Claudius would ride into the main courtyard on the bay-colored horse with the clearly marked star on its forehead. He would stay listening intently to everything Jesus taught. Martha always included him in the evening meal, although she knew having a Roman to dinner was not socially acceptable, and there were many disturbed eyebrows raised among her neighbors. The servant boys, however, loved Claudius's visits and made frantic scrambles to see who would get to water and feed the great stallion.

"Apparently," Martha leaned down toward Aaron, "you are on good terms with Claudius's horse?"

His face beamed his triumphal answer, and she suspected that "watering the horse" really meant "riding" him to the trough.

"Good!" she said, "because both you and Jude had better be just as fast and durable!" She shook her finger at him, and he responded with a smile to match the twinkle in her eyes. Privately she wished somewhat grimly that Claudius and his horse were standing before her instead.

"Yes, Mistress Martha. I'll get Jude."

As he disappeared through the inner curtained doorway, she called to him, "When you're ready, come to the house."

Joseph was not convinced as he listened to her conversation with Aaron; so he questioned, "Mistress Martha, in view of the difficulty in finding Jesus, are you sure they should go? I will go myself. The task needs a man."

"No," she smiled. "I really want you here, dear Joseph." As she rubbed at the fatigue in her eyes, she said, "Jesus should not be too hard to find as I know the general area where he's teaching. The thing that does concern me is the ugly rumors of death threats against him which are circulating out of Jerusalem. Jesus may not want to journey this way, but certainly that will not hinder the boys."

"But," countered Joseph, "the roads are so dangerous—filled with cutthroats and thieves. I fear for their safety."

Martha shook her head. "Oh, I think they will be swift enough, and two runners are safer than one. Now, do not fret about them as I want you to stay here. Besides, if my brother continues to improve as he has done this morning, I'll want you to help me take him outside or up on the roof for a little while. Remember," she continued, "the boys' love for the Master and their enthusiasm for some new adventure will have a way of making their feet exceedingly swift."

She was anxious to get back to her duties, so Martha left and said as she went, "You'll see, Joseph, they will find Jesus. In no time at all they will all come, and Jesus will be here!"

"I hope so, Mistress. I hope so," he said, not quite sure if he believed his own words.

Most of the servant girls were still sleeping, trying to catch up on several nights' wakefulness, but Naomi was too excited to sit down, much less sleep.

By the time Martha reached the cooking area, Naomi had stirred the sleepy fires in the bake ovens and had awakened them into bright coals. She was already elbow deep in bread dough when she stopped to look over at Martha.

"I am sending Aaron and Jude instead of Joseph. I don't know how long it will take the boys to find Jesus," Martha said as she sat down on a low stool. "Do we have any bread or cakes to give them as they run?"

Naomi nodded affirmatively, pulled her hands out of the big puffy gloves of dough, and said, "I've no bread, but I do have some cracknel cakes and plenty of dried apricots and figs."

After she dusted the last of the flour off her hands and arms, Naomi took several small grain cakes from a wooden cupboard, broke them apart, poured a little honey on each side, and stacked them neatly back together again. She selected the plumpest dried fruit from a woven basket tray and tied the whole thing up in a tidy satchel. The stiffness in her hands, Martha noticed, made her pace very slow, but the importance of the mission gave her great determination.

She finished tying it all up just as the boys came breathlessly through the door.

"Here," said Martha as she handed the satchel to Aaron. "This is to tide you over until you find Jesus." Then, smiling, she said, "Even Claudius's horse would need some grain for this task."

Holding the satchel and jiggling it up and down like he was

weighing the contents, Aaron looked at Naomi, smiled a shy smile, and said, "Thank you very much. We shall enjoy every bit of it!"

Then, serious all at once, he turned to Martha and said, "Shall we go straight to the temple in the city to find him?"

"No, I have heard that the Master is in the Perea area across the Jordan River and to the north. I understand he is teaching and preaching in those small cities up there. Since he attracts so much attention, it should not be too difficult a task to find him. However, if you have to ask someone if he has been to his village, do it with caution. He has his enemies. Please remember, haste is most important." The boys nodded soberly, their dark eyes dancing with the danger of their mission.

"Then," Martha continued, bending down to their eye level, "when you find him, give him this exact message. Say, 'Master, our mistress, Martha, needs you in Bethany. Please come as quickly as you can.' "

She paused, straightened up a bit, and, frowning, said, "No, no, not that. Just tell him simply, 'Master, the one you love is sick.' " She made both of them repeat the message to her and was pleased that they were as solemn as if they were taking a holy oath.

Those words will be enough, she thought. *Jesus will know, and he will leave instantly for the love of Lazarus. Even though he knows the danger, he will come straight to Bethany.*

"Now, be off with you," Martha said. Giving the boys a playful swat, she hurried with them as they left the back entrance. Then down through the side gardens, past the inner courtyard well, and to the main iron gates in the outer wall, which closed off the street, she half ran behind them. At the gate she touched both their shoulders and said, "The Lord go with you, my sons, and may He grant you the speed of fleeting deer." *Or Claudius's horse, whichever is faster, please, Lord*, she thought. They ran down the steep street, their sandals loudly clattering over the stones in the early hush of dawn, and she watched until even the sound was gone.

For some time Martha stood leaning against the gates just breathing in the warm peace of the morning. Nobody was about, and only a few early birds were chattering together. In fact, except for once, when she thought she heard Mary's voice calling her, the morning was as still and lovely as she had ever seen. She savored it deeply.

For a moment she considered going back to the house and resuming her duties, but the day was so beautiful, and she was so in need of a change of pace after the frantic past two days that she decided to walk downhill to her father's olive grove.

All the way down the street she reasoned that nothing was pressing. She was tired, and she felt she could well afford the luxury of not bestirring herself for a few moments. She didn't even bother to call Naomi. Martha simply pulled her shawl over her head and leisurely strolled down the hill, turned at the bottom to another steep hill, and quickly reached the wall surrounding the trees.

Josiah, her father, a man of practicality and intelligence, also had been blessed with a creative imagination. Their house, his business in Jerusalem, and this grove were all extraordinary feats to his credit.

Martha entered the grove through a small break in the stone dike wall and climbed back up the terraced hillside to the highest row of olive trees.

This is no ordinary grove, she thought and smiled. It was so much more. Even the stone walls which kept the land from slipping and sliding down the hill in the rainy season were planted with various vines and flowers. They were popping up here and there along the top. The olive trees themselves were healthy, fruitful, and, Martha thought, the most graceful of all trees except for willows. The crop was about five months away, but the trees were heavy with the feathery blossoms, and she knew the harvest would be extra special.

Between the trees, her father had planted rows and clumps of many different species of flowers. It was a splendid grove-garden. *More Mary's place than mine*, acknowledged Martha, but this morning it did not matter. *Lazarus was better—or was he?* Deep down on some hidden crossroad of her mind she remembered how, sometimes, a very sick person would suddenly sit up, take in nourishment, and his family would rejoice—only to watch in disbelief as he died that night or a day later.

"It is not good for me to dwell on these thoughts," she said abruptly, but bits and pieces of her memories clung stubbornly to her inner parts. Ignoring her deep feelings, she rationalized, "No, he is better—much better." But a part of her stood away from herself and said, "Why do you deceive yourself when you know better?"

The day is a day of beauty, the garden flowers are bursting into the spring air with a rainbow of colors, and I am determined to let nothing spoil the majestic peace this place gives to me, Martha said to herself. She absolutely gulped in the fresh, flower-scented air, and nothing had ever felt so good. *He is better,* she said over and over to herself. Still a part of her resisted the knowledge.

She made her way farther up to the corner on the upper hill and came to the tiny hut her father had built as a storage room for his tools. The hillside was watered by a small reservoir, and nearby was one of her father's ingenious clay pipes which supplied just the right amount of water. Martha sat on a low bench outside the hut and remembered all the times this grove-garden had been a playground for Mary and her. In fact, she remembered it was at this very spot, so many years ago, she had discovered her very own gift—her gift of healing from Jehovah.

Martha looked down at the clay pipe and a faint "ah, ha" broke into the morning.

It was that very pipe with its little trickle of water. *Right here is where my gift of healing all started,* she thought. *How old was I?* she stirred her memories. *Ah, yes, I must have been ten, and Mary just five. We played a game that day of hide and seek in this grove,* she remembered.

Mary had impishly run up the hill to hide behind the hut. She fell into a small grassy area between some bushes and the pipe and flattened herself against the ground to escape Martha's sharp eyes. Mary told her later that she was shivering with excitement as Martha came up the hill. But just as Martha had reached the hut, Mary spotted a plant by the watering pipe, and abruptly the game lost its significance.

"Martha . . . over here!" Mary had called. She jumped up,

giving her place away. "Come here and look . . . quickly," she urged. She was almost in tears as she parted the grass and showed Martha the plant.

Martha, breathless from the hurried climb, fearing a snake or some poisonous insect, laughed aloud with relief when she saw the plant.

"It's *not* funny." Mary's bottom lip formed a small pout, and her eyebrows pulled into a frown. "Someone has stepped on that plant. I can't remember what Father called it, but it has very special purple flowers on it. Now it's all broken. Will the plant die?" Mary's sensitive eyes and heart were full of concern as she questioned her sister.

Martha stopped her laughing smile when she saw how serious Mary was taking all this and said soberly, "Well, let me see if I can help."

Martha remembered her sentence about the plant that day was the first time she had actually put those words into the open, but it was not the last time, by any means. "Let me see if I can help" became her motto, her personal creed, and eventually her ultimate goal. It had all started in this grove-garden by the clay pipe, so long ago.

Martha recollected that she had lain down in the grass to get a better look at the plant. Instinctively, she pinched off a few of the most shriveled, yellowing stems, found a little piece of olive branch, and stirred the ground all around the plant. Then, cupping her hand by the pipe, she caught some water and carefully soaked the ground. After she had sent Mary to find a straight, short stick, she went into the hut for some strips of cloth. Mary finally found the right stick, "sturdy and tall enough," and Martha cautiously pushed it into the ground beside the main stem. Then she gently tied up the wilting plant with the strips of cloth.

"There, now," she said as she rinsed off her hands. "We'll come back and water it each day to see if it will grow again, little sister."

Mary's large blue eyes sparkled with obvious faith and confidence in Martha's ability.

Not more than three days later Mary's faith was confirmed.

She swooped into the inner courtyard, panting from her run and called, "Martha, Martha, come see it! It's beautiful. It's not going to die. *You saved it! You saved it!*"

Together the two little girls, picking up their skirts so they could move faster, dashed out the main gate, down one street, turned the corner, flew down another street to the break in the stone wall, and finally bounded up the hill to the pipe.

Breathlessly, Martha agreed. "It is a *beautiful* plant." By examining it closely, she saw the tiny new beginnings of one new leaf. and she flushed with a quiet pride. Her serious side would not allow herself to get overly jubilant, but Mary, on the other hand, had never known any such limitations; so off she ran to tell their father of Martha's gift. As Martha remembered it, Mary had told the whole village of Bethany that day.

She smiled at the clay pipe and this garden which held so many memories.

Martha could not bring to mind anything which suggested that she had used her gift of healing often after the plant that day. But two years later, when she was twelve, unexpectedly she picked up the gift again. It was almost as if her healing talents had been a buried treasure chest of gold and then suddenly were uncovered, unearthed, and ready to be spent.

On that day so long ago, her father had come home from his shop in Jerusalem and was getting the evening report from Joseph's father, Samuel, about the sheep herds and the terraced farmlands. It was a conversation which he savored slowly each night like a man rolling a good wine over his tongue. Martha always stood close, so she would not miss any detail.

Her father had not begun as a farmer or a sheep breeder. His expertise and source of wealth came from an exclusive and expensive shop which he owned in partnership with his brother and was located over the hill in the best trade-shop area of Jerusalem.

Between her father and her Uncle Tobias, they had built a handsome business dealing with imported artifacts and luxury household goods.

Martha loved to examine the new items in his shop, and once

n a while she and her sister were allowed to come and spend the
afternoon. Naomi would bring them. Martha would solemnly
gaze at the wondrous things, and Mary, as usual, would squeal
with delight over *anything* that had birds or flowers on it.

They both enjoyed looking at their own reflections in the
highly polished brass pieces. Martha loved examining the fine
filigreed lamps and lamp stands, while Mary was always drawn
to the fine selection of alabaster boxes and candlesticks. The
shop boasted such wondrous things as bedsteads carved out of
wood and inlaid with tortoiseshell or ivory (once they had one
inlaid with real gold), multicolored woven rugs from distant seaports, exquisite works of art, cashmeres and silks, and even
small heating braziers beautifully fashioned out of bronze. Their
house in Bethany held many similar treasures, but always there
was some new and exotic prize in the shop, and both girls liked
the idea of being the first to see it.

Her father saw the shop only as a convenient means to an end.
His first love, after Rachel and his children, Martha knew, was
not his shop or his buying trips to other countries, or all the
interesting merchants with whom he dealt. But his real love was
the land, the sheep, and especially the natural beauty of the hills
of Bethany.

As soon as her father had made enough money, he couldn't
move his family out of the noisy, bustling city of Jerusalem fast
enough.

He bought the choicest spot in all of Bethany, up on a high
vantage point with a view of the city. Their home had been built
to the eye-popping surprise of the townspeople. When it was
finished, Josiah and Rachel filled it with artistic furnishings.
Their pallets had carved wooden bedsteads. How that caused
talk. Martha laughed with the memory. There were handwoven
tapestries for the walls, thick, richly colored carpets for some
areas, and even low tables inlaid with other woods and ivory.
Martha's favorite table, which stood at one end of the great hall
by a couch, had a highly polished wooden top and was inlaid
with ivory. The ivory design was fashioned by a skilled artist to
look exactly like grapes hanging from a vine in a vineyard. All

their possessions produced many months of entertainment fo
the villagers as they gossiped and discussed the great house o
the hill.

Each day Martha's father worked in the city, took the shor
walk home to Bethany at night, and then questioned Bethany'
farmers and shepherds alike about the land and the lovely hills
He kept questioning the shepherds until he found Samuel, the
son-of-the-son in a long line of shepherds, who had no flocks o
his own, but worked for a hard-driving man in the next valley

Martha recalled that on the same day her father hired Samuel
he acquired Joseph, the son, and two plots of land. One acreag
spilled over two hills and was suitable for farming; the other wa
the grove she now sat in.

As her father's business continued to be blessed by Jehovah
Josiah took on more land. Soon he was well known for his ex
pansive wheat and barley fields. But his real fame sprang no
from his ability to direct the tilling of the soil, but of his expertise
in breeding and raising sheep. His herds had grown, and no on
could match the choice mutton and tender cuts of lamb or th
subtly tinted wool which Josiah and Samuel achieved by
crossbreeding.

Martha's reflections were interrupted by some deep stirring o
joy, and, surprising herself, she said aloud, "Lazarus i
better—really better." Then her thoughts returned to th
memories of her healing gifts.

Martha, on that day years ago when she was twelve, hac
listened eagerly as her father, Samuel, and Joseph talked about a
sick lamb. The lamb was special since it was sired by his bes
ram and born of his finest ewe. Joseph was telling her father hov
many different things they had used in trying to turn the fate
around for the lamb, but even his father had been unable to
suggest something. Nothing seemed to work in curing the ailing
lamb. The men nodded in disappointment.

"I thought this offspring would be near perfect," her fathe
had said sadly.

Martha had listened for as long as she could stand it, but afte
she heard "the lamb is so very ill" a third time, she gently broke

in with, "Father, where are the sheep grazing; I mean the herd with this sick lamb?"

"Over yonder," her father said, making a vague gesture with his hands towards the east.

"No, I mean where exactly. I'd like to go see the lamb. Maybe, Father, I could help." She did not see Joseph's annoyed look, but she did hear his low, guttural pronouncement of "How could *you* help?" He blurted it out before he could stop himself. Samuel burned a scornful look in his son's direction.

"Perhaps not at all," Josiah answered for her. "But that Martha cares and would like to go help pleases me." His answer to Joseph filled her with warmth, and she knew her cheeks were flushed and reddened in response.

Turning to Samuel and Joseph directly, he said, "The men of the village think my pride is my shop, my fields, and my herds, but this is not so. Standing before me, and two others in the house, are my real delights. They are my fields of pride, my herds of love, and because of them, I love life deeply and am a proud man."

Samuel nodded, but Joseph almost melted in mortification. He had not meant to demean the master's daughter; so he hurriedly explained, "Master, all I meant was . . . well, even my father, experienced in such matters had nothing to offer. How could a mere girl help?" Instantly he knew he had been foolish in his choice of the word *mere*. This time Josiah's look silenced him.

Her father sat down on a stone bench in the courtyard and said directly to Martha, "My daughter, the eastern slopes are not too far, and there are a few hours of daylight left. You really would like to see if you can help, wouldn't you?"

"Oh, yes, Father!" she fairly shouted.

Josiah looked at Joseph and said, "You will go with her." Joseph's *yes* was resigned, but without hostility.

That her father believed in her, though she was barely out of childhood, touched Martha deeply. In fact, she laughed as she remembered it, she was so thrilled about permission to go that she had been unable, for a change, to say anything. Leaving them in the courtyard, she ran off to get her things together.

With some help from Naomi, she filled a small goatskin bag
with yellow olive oil, took various herbs from her small pottery
jars, and carefully wrapped the blend in a linen towel. Naomi
found a clean cloth which could be used as a poultice or a plaster
if it was needed, and with that Martha was ready. She was a
picture of precision.

When she finished and came into the cooking area, Joseph just
stared at her. He found himself somewhere between marveling
at her confidence and scoffing at her lack of experience. When
she caught his skeptical look, she stated, "Everything in its time
and place, Joseph. That is as my father has taught me. We must
hurry, but we must not forget something and leave too hastily.
The lamb's life may depend on our thoroughness."

Joseph was only sixteen at the time, and he had never understood women anyway; so Martha especially puzzled him. She
was only twelve and always seemed to *know* what she was doing. Worse than that, she rarely made a mistake or ran out of
energy. Yet decidedly so, he had admitted privately to one of the
undershepherds that she would make a good working wife, even
if she did make him edgy at the back of his neck.

The two of them set off late that afternoon and found the
clusters of woolly animals with one of the shepherds holding the
ailing lamb.

She could not remember exactly what she had done with the
lamb, only that she and Joseph had brought it home, and because of Jehovah's gift to her, she had patiently turned the
apathetic bag of bones into a fat, energetic nuisance. Everyone,
she smiled with the memory, was annoyed with the antics of the
cured lamb, except her father. Whenever he saw the mischievous, woolly body, he would catch Martha's eye and solemnly
wink, remembering her part. The news of her success with the
lamb would have never spread outside the household, but as
usual, Mary told everybody.

As she sat in the grove, Martha chuckled and recalled, "That
sister of mine told just everybody!"

Martha remembered that slowly at first, but within a year, she
began to show up wherever there was an illness. By the time she
was thirteen, she had made the acquaintanceship of Mahalath,

Bethany's formidable midwife. Her desire to learn and her caring heart had helped her to brave the moment when she asked Mahalath if she could join her when the next baby was about to be born. Martha remembered the terror in her heart when the large, old woman had turned to her and spit out contemptuously, "You want to come with me to fill your eyes and head with gory sights so you can gossip about it later?"

"Oh, no, respected Mahalath," Martha answered. She was terrified, but she went on firmly. "I want to help with the suffering of others, and I want to learn from you." Before all of this had really penetrated the woman's inner places, Martha added, "I want you to be my teacher."

"Teacher?" Mahalath repeated the word carefully and bent down for a closer look at Martha. "I believe you mean it," she stated. "But you are forgetting who you are, girl!" the old woman said, scowling. "It is not proper for a daughter from the distinguished house of Josiah Ben Jochanan to dirty her hands with a midwife's business."

Martha's shoulders snapped straight, and she seemed to grow taller. Clearly she stated, "I am not in the least concerned with my social standing, and it matters not to me whether the villagers condemn or approve of me. I will not be bound to live by foolish traditions. I have a gift for healing, and I mean to learn about it and use it in all ways possible!"

Mahalath sucked in her breath so it whistled between the space in her two front teeth, and, peering down at Martha, she exclaimed, "Such a rare one, you are! I can see you are set in your thinking; so we shall see, Martha. You be ready, waiting, and we shall see." She went off waggling her head from side to side in wonderment.

Martha called to mind that she had almost exploded with joy at the thought of learning from the midwife. Then, to her surprised delight, it was only a week or so later when a small boy from a neighboring house stood at the front gate and yelled, "Mistress Martha shall come with me as Mahalath is ready to teach." *And ready she was,* mused Martha.

Her father hadn't been nearly so ready. It had taken Mary to convince him.

"It's just not done," Josiah said. His indignation showed onl**
by the agitated way he tugged on his beard.

"The Mahalaths of this world were born to be midwives. It **
right and good for them, but it is not for my daughter. We are **
distinguished family. Her dignity and reputation will be put int**
questionable repute if she pursues this . . . ."

He would have gone further with his stern rationale, but Mar**
put everything into its proper place. Her blue eyes were spar**
kling, wide open yet serious, and Martha thought Mary eve**
looked more beautiful.

"For some daughters, my father, you are right. It would pu**
their character in a questionable, even objectionable position**
but our Martha has a gift. Even from our childhood Jehovah ha**
blessed her with a special talent for healing. Remember th**
plants she restored and, of course, remember the ailing lamb sh**
rescued? Why shouldn't she learn from Mahalath? Perhap**
Jehovah has given her a gift for healing people and babies as we**
as plants and animals."

Mary finished, and Josiah meekly shook his head and nodde**
yes. Then smiling at Mary, he said in a voice loud enough fo**
Martha to hear, "What you're really saying is that this old ma**
must not tamper with the mysterious ways of God even if h**
comes from a distinguished family."

"Something like that, my father," she murmured quietly.

So, in the end, Josiah gave Martha his blessing, and even wen**
so far as to tell Mahalath to "teach Martha appropriately an**
thoroughly."

Mahalath took the charge seriously. No part of Martha's train**
ing was too obscure or too difficult. Every subject concernin**
childbirth was carefully covered. It was as if old Mahalath ha**
looked for a pupil all her life so she could leave her village o**
Bethany and the surrounding countryside in capable hands. Bu**
she'd found no one to take her place—until Martha.

Eagerly she spent many hours with the young girl, teachin**
her about the Hebrew value of having children. Once, when sh**
was telling Martha how wonderful it was to possess children, sh**
quoted, ". . . like the olive plants round about thy table: Behol**
that thus shall the man be blessed that feareth the Lord."

Interrupting her, Martha had asked, "Why have you no 'olive branches,' my teacher?" Her dark eyes were serious and grave with the question.

It was as if Martha had scraped a sensitive, festering wound, and the old woman caught her breath up in the hurt of it.

"I *have* this many olive branches," she said defiantly, holding up four fingers. Then, dropping her voice, she explained. "But as they came, God took them and replanted them in heaven with Him."

Abruptly, without any more explanation, Mahalath plunged into a whole set of rules for the woman with child.

Martha listened carefully to Mahalath as she sternly taught. "The expectant mother is not to take hot baths for fear of miscarrying. She is to develop the proper eating habits. She must avoid salt foods and fat." Martha's training went on and on. Mahalath had the list of herbs and other magical remedies to help and ease the time of confinement. She had rules to prevent miscarriage, potions for barrenness, and even advice for those having too many children.

It was all a heady and marvelous learning time, and each subject was covered long before Martha ever got to go with Mahalath to see an actual birthing. But by the time the old midwife allowed Martha to witness the big event, Martha was very ready.

Her brown eyes were wide open with an exciting amazement, and her admiration for the woman knew no bounds. She watched Mahalath ease the young mother from terrified, screaming anguish into a tearful, yet calm endurance. Then, a few hours later, she saw Mahalath catch the tiny bluish white infant in her ready hands.

In the quick time it took to see that the baby was a boy, he had lost his dead look, turned rosy pink, and finally his skin glowed a deep red.

His first cry was a cry of victory and a joyous salutation to the three women. Since he carried on a steady stream of cries, Mahalath pronounced him a "healthy olive branch." In her fiercely dedicated way, she washed him down and rubbed him with salt to prepare him for his wrapping in swaddling clothes.

Martha had not been too much help that day, for the chills stirred up and down her back and rendered her quite useless.

As Martha thought back over those days of learning, she guessed that the reason so many babies lived when Mahalath had been present at their births was possibly because of Mahalath's own deeply felt losses and her powerful desire to keep as many "olive branches" here on earth. She had been the best midwife anywhere, and now Martha knew the reason.

"Mahalath is gone now," Martha said aloud, and the words saddened her.

She sat in the garden realizing and appreciating the medical legacy the old teacher had left her. *How funny,* she reminisced, *I still get the same chills after all these years whenever a baby slips into my hands.* She sat pondering the times she had been Bethany's midwife and vividly remembered the moments when she had held aloft, for the mother to see, the precious, wet, squalling olive branch. How special she had felt standing there holding God's gift of life!

Suddenly Martha's warm memories were jarringly disturbed. It was as if her thoughts were being invaded by a loudly buzzing bee. She raised her head, listened, and heard another sound. The buzzing was louder and coming closer.

She could see a woman's figure running toward her through the trees. "Martha, Martha!" Her name was being called frantically. Now there were more bees, and their insistent droning was almost deafening.

Stiff with fear, Martha got up and began to run toward the approaching girl. She forced herself to go faster and commanded her rigid legs to move. Now, running and stumbling, she came through the trees, their low branches scratching her face, and she headed toward the figure. It was Leah.

Before Martha reached the girl, the bees stopped their buzzing. Her mind became suddenly still.

Then, from somewhere deep inside the marrow of her bones, Martha felt them—a hundred furious bees. Their stings burned steadily into her flesh, and she knew, even before she was told, it was too late.

Lazarus was dead.

4

NOT stopping on the hillside, but catching the girl's hand, Martha explained deftly, "I know, Leah. I know." Together they ran from the grove, their faces grim with the knowing.

Leah's voice, choking with tears, sobbed out as they ran, "When I awakened, Naomi had me take some lamb broth up to Lazarus. Mary had her head on his arm, and I thought they were just resting. But when she saw me, she told me to get you and said he was gone."

Martha slowed down their pace as Leah, between crying and running, could hardly catch her breath. Both women were aware of others on the street, moving and rushing towards the main gate of her house. *Word travels fast in such a small village,* reflected Martha as she appraised the crowd and nodded a silent greeting to those who were ready to give the day to mourning. Martha made sure her face was covered by the mask of calm confidence. However, the fury raging underneath was definitely out of control and completely hidden from the neighbors and friends who were quietly observing her.

Inside she was seething with angry fires.

There is no mercy, no justice today. Death is my constant companion. Yahweh, where are You? Have You abandoned me? Her mind was spilling out one accusation after another. *What was it King David had said?* She fiercely tried to remember the words of the psalm she had committed to memory so long ago, and suddenly the whole text filled her mind. The lines surprised her with their apt fitness for the hour.

> My heart is in anguish within me,
>   the terrors of death have fallen upon me.
> Fear and trembling come upon me,
>   and horror overwhelms me.
> And I say, "O that I had wings like a dove!
>   I would fly away and be at rest;
> yea, I would wander afar,
>   I would lodge in the wilderness.
> I would haste to find me a shelter
>   from the raging wind and tempest."

"I would give *anything* to fly away," she muttered as she reached her front gate.

"What did you say, my child?" Hannah asked. Her old face was lined with concern, and her voice was warm with tenderness.

"Nothing, Hannah," Martha said, putting her head down as she steered Leah past the small knot of women and into the main courtyard.

More words of David pushed into her mind as they entered the house and started for the staircase. The great room was already crowded with people, and to herself Martha voicelessly screamed:

> Save me, O God!
>   For the waters have come up to my neck.
> I sink in deep mire,
>   where there is no foothold;
> I have come into deep waters,
>   and the flood sweeps over me.
> I am weary with my crying;
>   My throat is parched.
> My eyes grow dim
>   with waiting for my God.

She reached the top of the stairs, and regaining some inner composure, mocked herself, and seethingly said, "Yes, David, I, too, seem to be 'waiting for my God.' " She began immediately to chastise herself for procrastinating so long in calling Jesus. Now it was all over. The Master hadn't reached Bethany in time, and the life of her brother had been spilled out, wasted, and once more the family sepulcher would mutely house yet another special love.

In Lazarus's room, everyone was resigned to simply wait for Martha. She felt slightly sick, and a coat of bitterness formed on her tongue. *If they only knew how unsure and unsteady I am, they would wait for someone else,* she thought tartly. *Don't they know I'm not their strong stone for leaning?* Still they were waiting, and she knew they were waiting for her. So she squared her shoulders, took a commanding breath of air, formed somewhere deep inside her a terribly intense determination, and strode into his room.

Naomi stood with Tabitha and Deborah just inside the doorway. Over by the window waited the sobbing Joseph. His back was toward the room, his head bowed, and his shoulders were shaking with his grief.

At first no one spoke, but then Mary, kneeling by Lazarus, sensed Martha's presence, uttered a small, anguished cry, jumped up to fling herself into Martha's arms, and overflowed with a rush of tears and words.

"He was so much better," Mary was talking and sobbing all at once. "You saw him, Martha. He *was* better. Then he asked me to sing. You know, like when we were children."

"Yes, like when we were children." Martha's tone was fragrant with bygone memories, and she hugged her sister closer.

"Then it was his turn. It was his turn," Mary dully repeated. She broke away and moved slightly to look down on Lazarus. "But, he was . . . ." Then dropping down beside his pallet, she cried out, "Oh, Martha, he is dead. We have lost him."

For the second time Martha replied, "Yes." And she repeated Mary's words, "We have lost him." She bent down and lifted her sister to her feet. While she brushed some hair from Mary's eyes and forehead, Martha's sense of duty returned. She said with quiet authority, "Now I must prepare him for burial. I want you to get Lazarus's alabaster box from the large closet in the lower chamber. Do you think you can do that?"

"Yes, of course, my sister." Mary wiped her face with a linen cloth. "Is there something else I might do?" she questioned as she reached the door.

Martha was standing by Lazarus's pallet. She looked down at him for a moment, then shook her head. "No, I think not," her words came out listlessly.

Mary disappeared, and Martha looked about the room. "Please go," she said with quiet dejection. Then, remembering, she added, "Joseph, I'll need some fresh well water, and, girls, you go with Naomi. She knows where the grave cloths are stored." No one moved; so she assured them that she was all right and she had much work to do if Lazarus was to be ready for burial by that afternoon.

Reluctantly they left with an inner denial keeping their pace slow and their walk stiff.

"Oh, Naomi," Martha called out, and the old woman lifted her head to catch each word. "I seem to remember seeing Hannah and Ruth in the courtyard. Ask them to come up and help me with this, will you?" Naomi shook her head and nodded yes as she left.

The window which earlier had let in the first rosy haze of dawn now shone brightly with sunshine. The tapestry was off to the side where Mary had hurriedly pulled it earlier, and the room was warming with the fresh breath of spring. Martha took the whole of the room into her heart and slowly examined the dear and familiar things.

The small carpets were exquisitely woven. Purposely she had selected the most colorful she could find to brighten up his room. The low, highly polished wooden table and matching reclining benches with their thick, scarlet silk cushions were comfortable yet sturdy and practical. On the gleaming white walls hung some imaginative but homemade tapestries. Martha had woven the basic cloths of linen flax into perfection, but Mary had embroidered them with tiny blue and brown birds and delicately wrought pink- and red-hued flowers.

The south wall was lined with cases for Lazarus's library. The large papyrus manuscript scrolls were carefully placed in the cases and numbered for quick access. Both Martha and Lazarus knew each scroll as if it were an old friend, for it was in this room Lazarus and she had learned to read. Only a select group of friends knew the extent of Martha's education, for educating a girl was simply not done by any Jewish family. Indeed, to learn reading and writing, Martha had to twist her father's arm, leg, *and* neck before he agreed. Even then the educating was done in this room *and* very secretly.

Education was available only for the male offspring. According to strict Jewish tradition, at age five a Jewish boy began studying. After learning to read and write, the boy was taught exclusively from the text of the Scriptures. Between the ages of ten and fifteen, he could go on to study traditional law or Mishna, and after fifteen, the pupil passed on to higher studies involving theological discussions.

So when they were very young, Martha recollected, their mother taught them some of the simple teachings of life, and by example they began to learn about their religious heritage.

When Rachel died, Naomi took up the teaching, dutifully carrying out all the ceremonies connected with the Sabbath, various festivals, and especially the Passover.

When Lazarus was a little past four years old, his father taught him a text of Scripture which contained some of the same letters which were in his Hebrew name. Both Lazarus and Martha had to memorize some of the psalms.

One of the rules of Jewish tradition said it was unlawful to live in a town where there was no school; so Josiah Ben Jochanan checked Bethany before he had their house built, and to his joy he found a small but flourishing school.

However, when Lazarus turned six and the time came for him to begin his compulsory education, he was not physically able to sit with the other boys in a semicircle around the teacher to learn.

Josiah had been torn with disappointment, but he determined in his heart that someway, somehow, his boy would study. No one in Bethany had heard of a teacher going to a pupil's house, but once Josiah thought of it, he did not rest until he had hired a young Jewish Pharisee as the boy's tutor.

At first, during the teaching sessions, Martha, having just

turned eight, wove little squares of cloth on a tiny loom and occasionally listened. She was only casually interested and stayed mostly out of curiosity. She loved watching the way the young man's dark-bearded face moved when he talked. Much of what the rabbi taught was written in the scrolls, but a greater part of his teaching was memorized; so he was forever talking. She was especially delighted when he was excited or reciting something to her brother, Lazarus, because the rabbi's beard made funny flopping movements.

No one knew, not even Martha herself, when the delighted fascination with the bushy black beard ended and the serious, attentive listening began. Certainly the teacher never dreamed the *girl* was learning all those afternoons, or as he said later, he would have doubled his fee.

In the years that followed, Lazarus learned the text of the Old Testament, starting with the Book of Leviticus and the other books of the Pentateuch. Later he went on to the Prophets and other books with Martha following close behind.

After Martha began catching on to the ways of reading, she persuaded her father with such supplication that her education could be invaluable to him in case, the Lord forbid, anything happened to him, especially in view of Lazarus's frail condition. She argued *someone* should be able to read and write in the family. It was clear, even in their early childhood, that Mary would be extremely creative and talented with her hands and would probably excel musically, but Martha had been blessed with other talents.

Both Martha and Lazarus loved reading and the challenge of writing, and they spent considerable hours learning and absorbing their skills. In fact, reading the scrolls and printing, first on astraca, which was broken pieces of pottery and easily obtainable, and then with reed pens on papyrus sheets, were some of the few things Lazarus could do without his fragile body becoming overly taxed.

Martha acted as his encourager and motivator, and together they spent as many afternoons as Lazarus could physically tolerate enjoying the manuscripts.

Josiah didn't exactly know what to make of Martha's education. Women who could read and write were virtually unknown in his Jewish circle of friends although someone he knew had heard rumors that Greek and Roman women were occasionally educated. He was mildly amused that his man-child had been taught his education, while his daughter had "overheard" hers.

Later on, Martha's theological questions *and* answers, as they lingered over the evening meal, were so challenging that Josiah sometimes forgot she was a girl. Once he found himself slapping her on the back when she had made an astute point as if she were an old and familiar crony of his.

Her intellectual perceptions and mental alertness were, in some ways, a mild embarrassment. "After all," he confided to his brother Tobias in their shop one day, "I'd hoped for great intellect from my son and, indeed, he has a fine mind, but from my daughter—ah . . ." and his voice trailed off. To Martha he had merely said, "You are a surprising package!" as he shook his head and finger lovingly at her.

Martha looked fondly at the wall cases holding all the scrolls and would have stood there longer, wrapped in the cocoon of her peaceful memories, had she not been startled by a discreet cough.

She whirled around to face Hannah and Ruth. Both women had helped with burial preparation before, and they rushed to her, embracing her with tears, not words. Martha was at once relieved and pleased with their willingness to help and their understanding stillness.

When they stepped back, Martha rolled up the wide sleeves of her wrinkled, soiled tunic, and, as if it were a signal, Ruth and Hannah attended to theirs.

Joseph, Naomi, and Mary all came, left their appropriate provisions, and, blinded by tears, wordlessly departed.

His entire body had to be ceremonially washed and cleaned; so with Ruth at Lazarus's head, Hannah on one side, and Martha on the other, they began their painful assignment. They worked as silently as the white, fleecy clouds that floated in the blue sky above their roof.

Martha uncovered Lazarus and busied herself by folding the thick coverlet. She placed it on the floor by the feet, and then gently, as if she did not want to awaken him, she slipped off the short undergarment she had put on him during the night, pulling it over his arms and head.

Now he lay before them naked and exposed. *The dead have no defenses, but then I suppose it doesn't matter*, she thought bleakly.

The modesty of Martha and the two women which forbade them to look upon nudity was set aside for the moment, and all of them gaped in disbelief at his collection of bones. Every part of him seemed to be held together by fragile patches of skin. Lazarus's eyes were nothing more than dark, sunken chasms, and his cheekbones protruded above his tangled beard. His ribs, like thin, bony fingers, showed clearly on each side of his chest. He was as white as marble except for the dark red scab-covered sores on his elbows, backside, and heels. Their eyes could hold no more; so they straightened up and pulled away. Instinctively they pulled their veils over their faces, for they were almost overcome by the sores' foul and pungent stench, which rose above him and hung between him and the women like an invisible shield.

Ruth was the first to return to the tasks. She turned and brought the first of many basins of water close to his head, while Hannah prepared the towels by his side. Martha began to wash him.

She touched his wispy, slightly matted hair and ran her fingers through his thin beard. Unsuccessfully, Martha tried to remember what it looked like before this last illness had devastated it.

Hannah kept her head down, avoiding anyone's glance, and Ruth's tears kept cascading down her face and splashing noisily into the basin, but very few words were passed among them.

Martha, solemn and dry eyed, imparted short, tight-lipped instructions only when it was imperative. She would have kept up her disciplined control, at least outwardly, as she finished bathing each part of his body, had it not been for the sight of the alabaster box.

Her father, Josiah, had given each of them their own extravagantly beautiful box containing precious burial ointments

Under the richly veined, white stone lid were four cloth-wrapped glass vials.

Martha's composure began to crack and shatter when, out of the corner of her eye, she saw the box on the low table where Mary had left it. However, after she undid the lid and broke off the end of the first vial and began spreading its highly perfumed contents over Lazarus's emaciated body, her calm gave way to utter chaos.

The potent, almost inebriating fragrance of the ointment, his body, now cool to her touch after being so fiery, the look of all his bones thinly disguised under his skin, and her overwhelming sense of loss all gathered together in a murky sea of grief and prepared to drown her. Martha fell across his body, and a fearful, terrifying darkness closed down upon her.

Somewhere in the dimness she thought she heard voices, and once she felt herself moving through the room, but the effort to speak was too great; so she lay submerged in her watery abyss.

"Martha, Martha, dear." It was Hannah bending over her and speaking louder than usual so Martha would hear.

"You are worn out. Just lie still and rest while we finish. You have not rested or eaten for so long that it is no wonder your strength fails."

It's true, Martha thought, making sense out of Hannah's words, but she tried anyway to get off the reclining bench. Firm hands stayed her and held on obstinately.

"When Ruth and I have finished, we will help you downstairs, but for now you must stay quiet." Hannah's words drifted in and around her, and Martha was too tired to protest.

By moving her head to the side, Martha could see the two women as they worked, winding the grave cloths around him. There was something wrong with his body, or was it the grave cloths? Martha turned her head away in the confusion of it all, and suddenly the memory of all the others she had wrapped paraded before her. The memories iced her veins with a chill, and even with her eyes firmly shut, she could clearly see Benjamin.

No, that's not Benjamin. It's Lazarus, her mind was spinning. Then she puzzled, *Am I dreaming or is that my love over there*

on the pallet being wrapped? Martha struggled to force her eye
open, but when the effort failed, she called out frantically, "Ben
jamin, my beloved, my husband, is it you?" The dream, o
whatever it was, did not change. She thought someone spoke to
her, but it was a muffled voice, and she decided the figure wa
Benjamin after all, and not Lazarus. He lay very still as sh
wrapped the cloth around his body.

She was fourteen the first time she had heard Benjamin'
name in connection with hers, and Martha had stiffened in
amazement! Her father and her Uncle Tobias were talking. They
were sitting on a rose-hued marble bench in the side gardens
under the shade of a large flowering vine tree, when she acci
dently came upon them and overheard her name. As it turne
out, they were conversing about—of all things—arranging a
marriage between herself and Tobias's son, Benjamin!

Martha knew, as did every proper Jewish girl, someday a
marriage would be arranged for her and for Mary, but somehow
she hadn't dreamed it would be this year—the year of her four
teenth summer.

Her body had become a woman two years earlier, and her
mind had awakened even before that, but there had only beer
shy glances to, or from, young men, including her cousin Ben
jamin!

For Mary it was a different jar of water, Martha clucked her
tongue knowingly. Every eligible son in all of Bethany and even
some in Jerusalem had seen Mary, and all wondered who woul
win her hand in marriage. No one had ever overlooked or ig
nored Mary's awe-inspiring face, her azure blue, angel eyes, the
sunrise color of her hair, or her dazzling smile which devasted
gloom and warmed even the coldest of hearts. "Now, me,"
Martha half smiled, "I have other avenues of talent." The reali
zation consoled her—but not much, nor often.

Many times she and Mary had seen Benjamin in Jerusalem,
both at the shop and in Uncle Tobias's home, but Martha had
said very few words to her young cousin. About the only thing
she knew for certain was that she was four years younger than
he and a half a head taller.

Even when the betrothal was announced in the synagogue,

nd she peeked out around the curtain which delineated the
women's section from the men's, she still couldn't believe what
both her eyes and ears told her.

"What frightens you, Martha dear?" her father questioned
her the day after the Sabbath. She was no withering, wilting
flower on a vine, but a strong girl; courageous and competent in
any situation, her father reasoned, but the betrothal and coming
marriage clearly filled her with dread—if not fear.

"I am not sure, my father," she responded, "but I think it is
the thought of leaving Bethany and living in the city." It was an
answer he could readily understand, for his love of the little
town of Bethany burned strong within his breast.

He smiled warmly and put a protective arm around her as they
walked down to the grove-garden. "I thought you might be worried about liking him—or even loving him," he smiled at her.

"No, you have often reminded me of the saying, 'Love comes
after marriage, not before,' even though it did not happen that
way between my mother and you," she said with a mischievous
smile playing around the corners of her mouth.

His ears turned an instant bright scarlet. "You never did miss
much, did you, my girl? Does that head of yours ever forget
anything?" he laughed as he asked.

"Not too much," she said, playfully ducking her head in an
attempt to be modest. "But I do know that when you left
Jerusalem one bleak, cold day on a camel caravan to buy
things in warm, sunny Capernaum, you came home with more
than the seaport's imported goods, Galilean handcrafts, and
sunshine! You came home with moonbeams and stars in your
eyes. Uncle Tobias told me of it."

"What else did that old rascal tell you?"

"Only that he could get no work out of you until you went
back and married the girl," Martha laughingly replied.

"So it was," said Josiah, grinning broadly. "It's true, our
life's union was not arranged by our families, although Aunt
Sarah had my cousin Dorcus all ready and eager. But you'll see,
Martha, this marriage between you and Benjamin will work out
exceptionally well. Perhaps even as well as your mother's and
mine," he added, trying to assure her.

Josiah continued because he thought she needed some added encouragement and said, "I've worked with him, you know." He leaned closer to her face as they walked through the flower beds in the grove. "While he is a bit reserved and quiet, he is a fine young man of honor and one who fearfully and respectfully worships Jehovah." Her father kept hoping his words would hasten Martha's acceptance of Benjamin, for he knew once *she* made up her mind things would go well.

"Father, it is not only the moving to Jerusalem which troubles me; it is something else." Here she hesitated, afraid of offending the dearest person in her whole existence, but he urged her to go on. So she blurted out, "It is just that he is, at times, so clumsy." She lowered her eyes and bent her head to escape her father's incredulous look as she knew she had to do some further explaining before he would reach any understanding.

"I don't know how many times I have stood by and watched him drop and break something, stumble over a stool, or misjudge the opening of a doorway," she explained. Her father was beginning to make a stab at understanding, but he still stood staring at her.

"You know me well, dear Father, and I have very little patience with someone like that. I admire a person who does things with accuracy, who doesn't waste time or have delays—like you, Father." She added the last words, hoping the truth would penetrate.

It found its mark, and Josiah threw his head back and gave a short laugh.

"My dear child, Benjamin is not like that anymore. It is true, though, when he first came to us at the shop, he was an overeager-to-please apprentice in selling, and he caused us much bewilderment. He was always bumbling about, and he did knock over a few things. Once his elbow reduced a finely crafted pottery vase, worth many silver talents, into a hundred tiny pieces." Her father clenched his fist over his heart as if the memory still pained him.

"But, Martha," he continued, "Benjamin has matured, and age seems to have smoothed out the unexpected thrusts and turns of his arms and limbs. In fact, his footsteps are as cautious and well placed as those of a young lion. He is not as you remember him.''

''I see,'' Martha replied gravely, meaning that what she could see was that the matter of her marriage had been settled, and she no longer had any real choice.

Two months after their conversation in the grove, the dowry settlement was agreed upon and paid, the slim ring of beaten gold given, and Martha, as she knew she would, married young Benjamin.

It was a wedding to be remembered, and no one who had been there ever forgot the day.

The noisy, ecstatic wedding procession, made up of young and old alike and headed by the nervous bridegroom, wound its way up the streets of Bethany to the bride's house. The hills rang of all the singing, dancing, and clowning which went on joyously around the pale-faced, colorfully dressed Benjamin. The festivities picked up considerably after they entered Josiah's courtyard. There, several young men added the beauty, and the noise, of four cymbals, two flutes, and one lute. Flowers were everywhere—spilling out of large jars, in garlands around the necks of the guests, or merely caught and held by waving hands.

The biggest commotion was in the people themselves. They were dressed in their finest rainbow-colored tunics, and their conversations were bursting with humorous tales and endless teasing. Their laughter, singing, and music floated into the house to Martha.

All morning her heart had pounded with vague fluttering of fearful expectation.

Martha had given in to Mary's insistent pleading and had used special ointments on her face and a heady perfume on her neck, but it was not to her liking or preference. She did it because it was simply easier to put it all on than to dampen Mary's enthusiastic cajoling.

Martha would have liked to have had some peace and quiet, but Mary was there constantly—noisy and bubbling like an early-spring brook. She brushed a sheen into Martha's hair and let it fall long and lustrous about Martha's shoulders as the bridal tradition decreed. Then, taking two front sections of hair from the center part, Mary brought the strands to the back of Martha's head and secured them with two gold combs. Skillfully her fingers moved precisely, and she wove tiny white flowers and fresh myrtle leaves into a fragrant wreath to crown Martha's dark, rich head of hair.

"You look as lovely as the rose of Sharon," effervesced Mary.

"I hope so."

Martha looked down at her dress and had to admit she liked it in spite of her edgy feelings. It was made of snow-white, imported silk that had been taken off the finest bolt ever seen in her father's shop.

Martha had fashioned it into a dress, but Mary with the help of Judith, Bethany's best seamstress, had inserted a breastplate of golden, woven fabric with an elaborate overwork of embroidered white flowers and tiny pearls. A gold sash completed the dress and matched the delicately made bridal sandals; so except for her veil, she was ready. "At least I look like I'm ready," Martha ventured.

She was still fidgety and concerned with her appearance, or was it just everything, when both girls heard the bridegroom's procession clamoring outside and knew the time had arrived.

Two young friends, Elizabeth and Vashti, came bounding unceremoniously through the doorway.

"He's here. Everyone is here . . . ."

"Oh, Martha, your dress is beautiful."

Both girls, dressed in white, had been chosen along with Mary to serve Martha as bridal maidens, and their happy chattering reflected their high excitement over the honor.

Impatiently Elizabeth and Vashti waited while Mary arranged Martha's robin's-egg blue veil over her head and shoulders. Then with heads held high, they all escorted her to meet Benjamin. The girls passed the servants, who, approving, nodded and voiced their "ahs." They walked through the throng of people to the place of honor. The beautiful Grecian chair, surrounded with huge bronze pots filled with flowering tree branches, stood alone at the end of the room waiting for the intended bride and her maidens.

Martha sat there like a young queen waiting for her king. But
en when her father, Josiah, kissed her forehead and whispered
e was beautiful, it did not assuage her terror. Her feeling of
diculousness was unparalleled to anything she had ever felt in
r whole fourteen years of living.

Benjamin's eyes avoided hers. Even on their hilarious,
ention-getting walk from Bethany to his parents' house in
rusalem, they remained close to each other, but their eyes
ver met.

Nothing it seemed, not even the extravagant ceremonial feast
rved to them under their special wedding canopy, the gifts
vished upon them, nor the lengthy blessings of the many toasts
ade to them complete with a heady, rich wine, could bridge
eir souls or entwine their hearts together.

Later, when Martha had been led to the bridal chamber by
ary and the other maidens, she sent them away without ac-
pting their help to undress, and motionlessly she sat on the
uch. She had only hints of gossip, unwillingly overheard in the
arketplace, to prepare her for the rigors of womanhood on this
uch, and she absentmindedly traced the bedding's design and
tterns with her fingertips and fearfully considered the next
urs.

Martha smiled now in her dark place of dreaming and remem-
red how needless her fears had been.

Benjamin—dear, gentle Benjamin—had finally come in to her,
t so hesitantly, so haltingly, and so filled with his own fears
at almost instantly she warmed to him. He was not trembling
om desire but from terror. With only a small glance at him to
se the moment, she unwound her veil and laid it aside. In the
zy glow of the small lamp above them, Benjamin perched
rvously beside her, and his eyes were filled with quiet obser-
tion. When she had removed the tiny gold combs from her hair
d the last of the wilted flower crown, he reached over and
sitatingly touched her rich, brown hair which cascaded around
r shoulders. Its softness surprised him. It even gave him the
urage to touch her face, but when he took her chin in his hands
speak to her, the smoothness of her skin and the deep, rich,
own of her eyes surprised him even more. He had never really

looked at her before, but now—here, alone, and together—
found a loveliness which at once was as bewildering as it w
wonderful. He wondered what other surprises were in store f
him with this one.

"I am afraid that I shall, in some way, hurt you by this night
Benjamin softly explained as he held Martha's face gently in h
hands. "I've no experience with a woman," he confessed, "a
sometimes I am, well, you know—clumsy."

Martha took his hands from her face and wordlessly be
down before him. After she removed his sandals and her ow
she stood up, slipped off the dress with its golden sash, a
carefully laid it and all her undergarments on a low bench. Whe
nothing more hid her ivory-colored skin, she turned and face
him without shyness.

He sat quite still, watching her with unconcealed wonde
ment. And when he said, "Martha, in our shop I have seen ma
beautiful things, but nothing will ever be as beautiful as what
have just witnessed," she more than willingly stepped over
him and yielded herself to his arms.

On their couch, in between their whispering and his kisse
Martha heard him say, "I pray I am not being clumsy."

She had never known or dreamed such delirious joy was o
tainable for mere mortals of this world. As her body relinquishe
itself to his touch, Martha pressed her lips against his ear ar
rather fiercely whispered, "Oh, no, my love, you are n
clumsy!" Nor was he.

Less than two new moons later, the bubble of newly foun
euphoric joyousness burst and shattered before her horrifie
unbelieving eyes.

Benjamin and her father had been standing on a busy street
Jerusalem's bazaar talking with another merchant when
horse-drawn chariot, minus its Roman centurion drive
careened with the speed of a whirlwind, dragging, whirling, ar
scraping both her father and Benjamin to death under a fury
hooves and sharply spiked wheels.

Sometimes Martha could still hear their screams, but at th
moment all the space in her mind was filled with thick silenc
"Oh, dear Adonai, am I seeing a vision? Is this happening or a

having a dream?'' Martha wondered. And then with tenacity she struggled to surface up through the misty haze, but all that would come clear were the pictures in her mind of the mutilated bodies of her husband and father. Martha remembered they had lain very still as she washed and wrapped them that day. "Yes, as still as Lazarus today," she whispered as she spiraled and slid backwards and downwards into her black, silent, and dreamless chamber.

Nor did she awaken or feel herself being carried down the stairs in Joseph's sturdy arms.

5

MARTHA felt she had been sleeping for days, but when she awoke in her own room, she found she was still dressed in her dirty, stained dress. The nightmare of being awake flooded her mind with its very own special horror.

Martha guessed by the sun's low, afternoon pink glow that it had to be about the tenth hour. "Lazarus must be buried before sundown, or the decay will begin," she said aloud as she raised herself up from her pallet with a sudden start of realization.

The door to her room opened, and Mary appeared with a basin of fresh water. Seeing that her sister was sitting up, she gave a small sigh of relief and said, "Oh, Martha, you have awakened! Good! I was about to get you up as it is time to . . . ." Without finishing, Mary put the basin on a wooden chest, and then helped Martha up off the pallet and out of her tunic.

Holding the garment away from her, Mary observed, "It is so crusted with soil, it could stand alone." Then, with the tunic still at arm's length, she hurried out the doorway.

Martha washed and drew enormous strength and refreshment from the cool water. She dipped her towel in and out of the basin, letting its coolness bathe the fire out of her face, her body and her soul.

From the closet Martha found clean undergarments, her best black tunic, and her opaque black veil. Carefully she dressed and as she finished, she brought out from a drawer her dark maroon sash and tied it around her waist.

When Martha surveyed her dress, she caught a glance of her hair in the polished bronze mirror and knew it was beyond even Mary's help. Quickly she undid it and was giving it a hurried brushing when she heard a new commotion above the mourners' wailing. Something was happening in the kitchen area. She could not tell what. Martha divided her hair in three sections and expertly plaited it into one thick braid. By the time she had wound the braid at the nape of her neck and secured it with several pins, Mary and Naomi, followed closely by Joseph, almost tumbled into her room.

"What is it?" she mumbled, still holding one pin in her mouth.

"It's the boys, Aaron and Jude. They have returned," explained Mary.

"Oh, good," Martha said matter-of-factly as she put away her hairbrush and wiped up the remaining drops of water from the basin.

"At least Jesus will be here when we bury Lazarus," Martha said and then became puzzled because she sensed something was amiss.

"Why are you standing there? Why are you not out meeting him? Go fetch him! He is our guest," Martha charged. Sometimes their lack of hospitality was a deep thorn in her flesh. Stamped clearly on Martha's mind was the memory of the large feast she had given for Jesus and his disciples. She had been well cautioned about her thoroughness in serving that night and yet she still maintained that nothing should disturb the common courtesies of hospitality.

When none of them moved, Martha commanded, "*Go* and greet the Master as he comes."

"That is just the problem." Mary shook her head as she spoke. "He is not here. He is . . . is not even coming."

"Not coming?" Martha stared at her sister. "What do you mean—not coming?"

Without waiting for an answer, Martha pushed past them, out her doorway, across the short hall, toward the cooking area and called out loud and strong, "Aa-ron and Juu-de, come here!"

She needn't have yelled. They were standing in the middle of the room, their tired, dirty, and obviously tear-streaked faces turned up, awaiting Martha's predictable scorn. That they had failed in their adventuresome mission was one thing; to face Mistress Martha and explain was quite another.

"Well?" Martha bent over with hands on her hips and searched their faces.

"We went up across the Jordan and into Perea as you told us and we found the Master." Fatigue and fear raised Aaron's voice a tone higher than usual.

"We went to *three* villages before we found him!" Jude offered as argument in their behalf, as they desperately wanted to please her.

"Did you go to him straightway and give him my message?" demanded Martha.

"Yes, we did!" It was Jude for the defense again. "And it was not easy! His disciples, many other men, and a whole group of Pharisees were all crowded in around him. We pushed through anyway and asked permission to speak with him."

"But did you give him my exact message?" Martha questioned.

"Yes, Mistress Martha," Aaron bowed his head wearily. "I said, 'Master, the one you love is sick.' "

"Well?" Martha pushed.

"Mistress, Jesus did not say anything. He just sat down on a stone courtyard wall, bowed his head, and covered his face with his hands."

Then Jude picked up the story.

"Andrew knelt down beside Jesus and said, 'Our friend Lazarus has been sickly since he was a babe. Will he die now?' "

"Yes, go on. What did the Master answer?" Martha pressed impatiently and bent closer to catch each word.

Aaron continued, "Ah, Jesus just looked up at Andrew, and then to all of us he said that the purpose of Lazarus's illness was not unto death but for the glory of God. Then he stood up and said, so everyone could hear, 'I, the Son of God, will receive glory from this situation.' " Aaron's shoulders squared a bit as he repeated Jesus' words.

"Oh, that is *just fine!*" Martha fairly snorted. "Our brother is dead—not ailing, but dead—and Jesus says his illness will not end in death, but in *glory?*"

Her thoughts whirled within her. *Jesus always talks in riddles*

*nd rhymes. I wish he would speak plainly. I wonder if I shall
ver understand him. I do not know why he speaks as he does!*

Returning her penetrating gaze to the boys, Martha prodded
again. "What happened next?"

"Nothing," Aaron gestured helplessly with his palms turned
upward.

"Nothing?" exploded Martha. "Just like that? Nothing? Did
he not give you a message for me or speak personally with you
boys?" Her eyes were wide with incongruous wonder.

"Oh," nodded Aaron, remembering. "He bade us eat and
sent us on our way back, but he did not send any message or
say if he would come at all." Martha's expression had not
changed; so Aaron added, "We did our best, Mistress Martha."

"I think it was Master Andrew," Jude volunteered, "who
asked Jesus if they would all come directly to Bethany, and
Jesus just said, 'Not now.' "

Martha silently opened her mouth and formed the words "Not
now?"

What does it all mean? She shook her head as her exasperated
thoughts kept coming. *We love Jesus. He is our friend. We have
asked nothing of him before. He is such a puzzling, mysterious
friend,* her thoughts surged on. *He is godly and quite literally
filled with heavenly power like the prophets of old. Yet he walks
among us, eats with us, and is so amazingly human that I sometimes cannot envision him as the Messiah.* Then, aloud, to cover
her hurt, Martha blurted, "He is such a mystery!"

Mary, still standing in the doorway, said softly, "My sister,
our Lord must have his reasons."

Martha whirled around and, shaking her head at Mary, flung
out, "Oh, yes, I am confident he has his reasons, but just try to
make any sense out of it! I wager even you, sweet Mary, cannot
figure why he has not come to aid us or comfort us in our sorrow!" Martha's words were seething with the fires which were
burning inside her breast.

Even as she spoke, Martha silently observed that the fires
within her seemed to burn hotter and more frequently than ever
before. It was a trait she did not like in herself. *I seem to be
angry from sunrise to sunset,* she reflected, almost startling her-

self. She mentally shook herself free from the guilt of it, assuaging her soul by thinking, *The Lord knows I've sufficient reason to be angry!* But still the fires and hurt did not ease or go away.

The sound of the mourners' weeping and wailing in the main room of the house returned Martha's sense of priorities back into focus. Quickly she assumed her rightful leadership position and pushed down her heated thoughts and searing hurts.

In spite of herself, her condition, and her frustration, Martha had the presence of mind to realize that the boys standing before her were tired, hungry, and still wearing their dirt-clogged sandals. Once again her high sense of hospitality won over her feelings. Almost roughly she steered Aaron and Jude to some wooden stools and began working loose the crusted leather straps of their sandals.

When she handed their shoes to them, she said pleasantly, "There now, you go with Joseph and get washed. Aaron, wash that blister on your heel and rub it with oil. Then bind it up with a cloth." To both boys, she continued, "After you've changed your tunics, come back inside. I'll have Naomi get you some barley soup and bread. I'm sure you are both weary; so after you've eaten, you may take your rest." She ruffled their hair and dismissed them with, "You did well and earned the rest."

Out the door they went, but Martha, catching Joseph's arm, said, "One moment, please." He stopped, turned, and faced her.

"I just realized, we will have to rearrange the bodies in the tomb if there is to be sufficient room. We will have to use the ossuary. After you help the boys, I'd like you to take several men," she motioned her head toward the courtyard, "and transfer the remains of my mother from the stone bier to the ossuary."

Joseph nodded his head in understanding and knew what he must do, but he felt a flush of relief when he heard Martha add, "And I shall come with you."

Later, as the boys were eating, with Mary and Naomi hovering over them, Martha, Joseph, and several men left the house. The men carried the small carved stone ossuary box up the hill to the family tomb.

Josiah Ben Jochanan's tomb, or sepulcher, as some called it, as a private burial place befitting the distinguished family. It d been dug out of the rocks on the side of the hill. The stone overing the entrance was shaped roughly like a door. The stone atters had left it naturally rounded on top, but it was flat on the ottom to keep it from rolling. They had chosen a rock deeper an a man's arm in thickness. It took four of the strongest men Bethany to move the massive stone aside.

Martha smiled sadly in spite of her sorrow when she heard one an softly curse and say, "I think it would be easier to move vo sleeping camels than this thing."

When the stone gave way to the men's insistent pushing, Martha stood straight, with head up, waiting for the dank, musty r, which she knew would float out to fill her nostrils.

The men stood mutely by the side of the entrance while oseph took Martha's arm, and the two of them entered the epulcher.

The inside of the tomb was exactly as she had remembered it: mall and square in design with large hewed-out niches in the alls and two benches, one on either side of the entrance. The naller wrapped figure on one bench was her mother; on the ther side, her father.

As she stood looking at the bodies, Joseph left her for a mo-ent, and when he came back, he and another man carried the ssuary inside. They set it down and carefully lifted off its heavy one lid.

"Which one?" Joseph looked at Martha, not remembering.

"My mother," she said, pointing to the body. Then slowly the vo men gathered the fragments of cloth and bones off the bench nd with respect and tenderness, placed them in the ossuary. Then the lid was securely in place, they lifted the box and arefully placed it in one of the niches.

With the bench ready for the newest body, Martha sighed, nook her head in resignation, and then walked back with the nen to the house for Lazarus. It was a quick, silent trip down ne street to her house.

When they reached his room, Joseph and two men placed the rapped and covered body of Lazarus on a narrow wooden

frame which was latticed together by leather straps. Using th
as his bier, they carried Lazarus out of his room. Mary join
them, and down the stairs they went, past many tearful face
out into the courtyard. Then, with most of Bethany's villa
people following close behind, the procession slowly made i
way up the steep hill to the sepulcher.

Martha and Mary, their black mourning veils securely ov
their heads and faces, walked arm in arm a few paces behind th
bier. Their anguished tears ran unobserved and freely down the
faces. They had always known this sad day would come; y
neither was really prepared for the cold hand of sorrow whic
tightly clutched their hearts.

At the tomb there was no ceremony or burial ritual. Lazarus
remains were simply placed on the prepared and waiting benc
The Rabbi Ben Isaiah offered a short, open eyed prayer endi
with "Almighty Jehovah, give us understanding hearts and me
ciful wisdom in our time of deep sorrow."

The sisters bent over, touched his form to say their fin
good-byes, and then stepped out of the tomb without a backwar
glance.

Joseph and several other men groaned and strained against th
massive stone, but with a final heave, the stone settled int
place. As the men dusted off their hands and clothes, it marke
the end of the funeral and signaled the time for the villager
condolences to be voiced.

Martha heard them; yet she didn't. It was as if what they we
saying was all muffled and subdued. What she could really hea
loud and clear, was her own overwhelming questions abo
Jesus. *Why did he not come and heal Lazarus before it was to
late? Why?*

Hannah's arm was around Martha's shoulder. Dorcus had or
of her arms; Ruth, the other. All three women were saying all th
comforting things one always says at times like this, but Marth
shut them out and could only question, *Why, why, why?*

As the procession wound its way back down the hill, the rab
pushed in between the women to take both Martha's and Mary
elbows in tow.

"You know I am a Pharisee," he said, over the crying an

oaning of the mourners. Yes, the women automatically moved
eir heads up and down.

"Then, you know I believe in personal immortality. I believe
the resurrection and that we shall see Lazarus again." His
oice had a funny kind of cheerfulness in it—almost as if he were
aying the words so that *he* might be reassured.

Martha peered out at him through the blackness of her veil.

"You'll see . . ." Rabbi Ben Isaiah went on. "You'll see him
Judgment Day, and the whole of Josiah Ben Jochanan's fam-
will be restored."

Neither Martha nor Mary responded. They simply walked
ong, each wrapped in her own cloak of confusion, aware only
the gaping holes in their lives because of their losses.

6

SCREENING her face with her dark, heavy veil, Martha gave her full attention to the sand-colored cobblestones passing beneath her feet as she walked home.

The rabbi continued his endless stream of comfort. "The psalmist has written," he said, " 'Such a man will never be laid low, for the just shall be held in remembrance for ever.' "

Martha absently nodded and remembered a passage in Proverbs which reads, "The memory of the just is blessed: but the name of the wicked shall rot."

Our Lazarus was that just and righteous man, she thought, *and his memory is blessed, but I shall never stop loving or missing him.*

She turned her attention back to the rabbi, for he was saying, "If there is no resurrection, then there's no hope beyond this life."

Mary's eyes, red-rimmed from weeping, met the rabbi's gaze, and he continued, "A nation without hope, my child, is like a night without stars. And we do have hope, the blessed hope of eternal life."

He warmly encircled both women with his arms, and they continued their slow walk homeward.

When the procession of mourners reached the last turn in the street, Martha lagged behind Mary and the rabbi and purposely slowed her gait, letting others pass, until she stood alone.

The rabbi had picked up his one-sided discussion and was so absorbed in his own world of rhetoric involving his beliefs in the Judgment Day and the resurrection that he and Mary had almost reached the iron gates before he missed Martha.

Turning around, he looked back up the street into the dusky pink sunset and called, "Martha? Come."

"In a moment, Rabbi. In a moment," she answered.

"Are you alright?" Mary called.

Martha shook her head affirmatively and waved them on.

She was in absolutely no hurry to join them or even, for that matter, was she willing to listen to them as they consoled her. Desperately she wanted to deny this whole day, to put it out of her head so she would not have to deal with the painful, frustrating questions it had presented.

Martha had stopped in a favorite spot. From where she was standing in the street, just after the last turn, she could look down a short distance and see Josiah Ben Jochanan's magnificent house—her house, the house everyone called "Martha's." To her it was not Martha's house, but the house of her father, and she never tired of the splendid sight.

She stood alone as if she were a stranger to the area and watched the mourners moving by the front wall and entering through the intricately scrolled iron gates. Finally she gave her full attention to the stone dwelling beyond the gates and the people.

The great house had been built to her father's precise instructions, and because Josiah was both wealthy and well traveled, his home and furnishings reflected Roman, Greek, Hebrew, and even Assyrian cultures. In any case, the house was a far cry from any typical or common Palestinian residence.

When Martha was little, she pretended their house was really a luxurious king's palace and, indeed, to many of Bethany's townsfolk, it was exactly that. The size of the stone buildings alone substantiated Martha's pretending and the villagers' surmising.

Martha lifted her veil off her face and laid it on her head. By squinting her eyes she could block out people, plants, trees, and other distractions, to see the house more clearly. She stood lovingly taking in the great structure. Actually, her home was more like three stone houses than just one, she observed quietly to herself.

The wide back building was two floors tall and flat roofed. Its

windows were crisscrossed with delicately wrought wooden lat
tice work.

She could see that the richly carved cedar wood entrance
doors had been flung open, and people were making their way
inside. Each day for several weeks the massive doors would be
open as word of Lazarus's death would travel over the countryside and mourners would come to pay their respects. Because
Lazarus was so well loved, Martha knew any time alone with her
grief would have to be postponed for a while.

She returned her full attention to the house. The main back
section, its white stone now a deep orange from the setting sun,
was flanked on its eastern and western sides by single-storied
buildings which jutted out toward the street, forming a deep
center courtyard.

Martha watched the people. They moved around the well in
the courtyard, the trees, the shrubs, and on into the house, and
she knew she could not linger too much longer. She would have
to join them soon, but the sight of the house held her for a
moment more.

The house, outer walls, and gates were all bathed in the dusky
glow of early twilight. She could still see some glimpses of color
in the courtyard. The trees were abloom with spring's first
leaves, and here and there the masses of flowers against the
black mourners' robes and the cool, whitewashed stone house
were like splashes of color on a tapestry. Dearly she loved the
house and gardens. "Perhaps," she said aloud, "I love this
house because it is the one thing in my life which remains constant. It does not change, go away, or die."

"Martha?" It was Hannah. She cupped her hand to her mouth
and called from the gate, "Martha, you must come now. Everything is ready."

"Yes, I guess it would be," Martha responded to herself. She
called down to Hannah, "I'll be right there." She knew in the
short time it took for the company of people to reach the
sepulcher, bury Lazarus, and walk back home, busy hands
would have gathered special dishes of food together for the
mourning family and friends to feast upon.

Martha embraced Hannah at the gate, and as the two women

ntered the main hall, Martha was not surprised to find every-
hing attended to and definitely ready. What did surprise her was
he manner in which she was treated. For suddenly Mary was at
er side and both of them were escorted through the groups of
eople in the main hall of their own house as if they were hon-
red guests or the governor of the feast.

Some mourners were standing clustered about in groups.
Others were moving quietly among the gathering of friends.
Even as she walked, she inhaled the deliciously fragrant aromas
f an abundance of prepared food.

Here and there both sisters stopped briefly to say a word or
wo to the many friends assembled there. Martha's cooking abil-
ty and sense of smell combined at one point, and she distinctly
dentified the scent of baked quail. She guessed the fowl had
een given by Nathan and Anna who lived on the edge of
Bethany. They took special pride in their assorted birds, and
heir success in keeping chickens, geese, quail, and partridges
vas second only to the perfect way Anna spit roasted them.

Rebecca and Dorcus stood before the sisters with a basin and
owel. Hannah guided them to a couch. Hesitantly, because
isually in this house she was the hostess, Martha sat down
ingerly beside Mary as Hannah and the others washed her feet.

When that task was performed, Hannah led them from the
reat hall, through an archway, and into the long dining room on
he eastern side of the house.

Mary glanced at Martha and with a soft smile said discreetly,
"One would think we did not know where the table is here in our
wn house."

"I was just thinking about that," Martha replied.

Between greetings and friendly but subdued salutations,
Martha took in the large rectangular room with its dark
ycamore-beamed ceiling, its gleaming white walls, and its
ighly polished table and noted with some degree of pleasure
hat the room was exactly as it should be. Everything was in
rder, and someone had done everything right—without her.

In each of the four corners the tall lamp stands were brimming
vith flaming oil, illuminating everything very well. The long, low
able, surrounded by its reclining couches which looked like the

spokes of a wheel, was crowded with food dishes. The foo
seemed to pick up its own special glow from the two candelabr
wedged in between trays and plates on each end, and the sigh
made Martha ravenously hungry.

There was such an abundance of food that someone had re
moved the bronze urn which usually graced the table as a cen
terpiece. Martha didn't have time to question its whereabouts a
Hannah took her arm. Both Martha and Mary were led directl
to the center couches of honor on both sides of the table.

Martha felt an uncomfortable, almost foolish shiver run up he
back as she settled down on the very couch she had led honore
guests to during past evenings' meals.

Most homes in Bethany did not have a separate eating place
The people simply took their meals at small, low tables and sa
on wooden stools in the common rooms of their homes. Cer
tainly no house boasted upholstered reclining couches, and lon
ago there had been a great deal of speculation in Bethany as t
Josiah's whys and wherefores of eating.

Actually it was all quite simple to Josiah. He had made buyin
trips to many foreign cities and seaports. In the process, once o
a trip to Rome, he had been befriended by a wealthy art mer
chant. Several times Julius Marcos had invited Josiah to take hi
evening meal with the Marcos family, but Josiah had alway
gracefully declined. Finally, Marcos's persistent, kind invitatio
and Josiah's own loneliness won out. Josiah swallowed his fear
about the "barbarous" Romans and their nonkosher foods an
gratefully, if not a bit apprehensively, accepted.

He was pleasantly pleased to find that the shrewd busi
nessman, Julius, was at home, a warm and gentle family man
He was quick to note that Julius understood his concern abou
Jewish dietary laws, for the food that was served was good, ye
plain and very much in keeping with Jewish tastes. Josiah fe
more than a few pangs of guilt over his former inflexible attitude

Josiah was even more pleased when at the first dinner h
found that affluent Romans ate in a separate room made just fo
eating, but he was almost joyous to find that they ate their meal
at a triclinium. Josiah never stopped marveling about how nice
was to lie down on couches and eat!

He had said to Martha after returning from the Rome trip,
You know, Martha, the Roman occupational army rules us and
ur land with an oppressive, heavy hand; but we can learn from
em in some ways."

Even though she was young, Martha had heard horror stories
f Roman atrocities and torturing, and her prejudice and con-
mpt for all Romans ran high within her.

Disdainfully she asked, "What could Israel's chosen people
ossibly learn from those heathen barbarians?"

"For one thing," Josiah stroked his beard, "we could study
eir water system with its aqueducts, cisterns, and clay pipes
d also the way they build their houses and take their meals."

"Take their meals, Father?" She had looked at him, her
own eyes popping with the wonder of how he knew of their
ays.

"Yes . . . take their meals," he repeated. Then he told her all
out the Marcos family, their dining area, and their couches.
e had found that Roman women ate with the men, and Josiah
ked that whole idea much better than the Jewish tradition of the
omen eating by themselves in the women's quarters.

"Just think of this, my daughter," he gestured with his hands.
In the house of wealthy Romans, everyone takes his meals in a
om dedicated to the purpose of eating. The table is low, and
erpendicular to the table are the reclining benches or couches.
ou simply lie on the couch on your left side, head towards the
ble, and eat as usual with your right hand. It is both practical
d pleasant!"

"Ah, yes. Practical and pleasant. I've seen Adoniram's cows
clining in the fields, chewing away at their cuds, and that is
xactly how they looked—practical and pleasant."

Martha smiled to herself as she remembered because here she
t on a couch in the very same room her father had designed for
em. It was a Marcos room to her, and she had come to love it
s her father had.

This night they were using all the couches and had added as
any stools as the room would allow so most everyone could eat
gether.

The table talk was low, intimate, and friendly; yet it was not

easy for Martha to wholeheartedly enter into things. It wa
especially difficult to remember she was, at this feast, a guest
She looked across the table at Mary and admired the way he
sister could open up her heart and mouth with such grace. Mar
never seemed to have any trouble listening and aptly comment
ing. Tonight Mary was responding graciously to each person
and Martha was even more aware of her own stiff responses.

"I would be much more comfortable standing and servin
with Tabitha and Leah than lying here all 'practical and pleas
ant,' " she muttered to herself.

When she had first smelled the luscious aroma of baked quai
she had been instantly hungry, but once at the table, she lost a
desire to eat and absentmindedly picked at her food. Listlessl
Martha took a bite of pale yellow cheese, dipped a cris
cucumber slice into the wine vinegar and oil bowl, noting it
freshness, and even bit off a tasty bite of baked quail, but sh
had no appetite or incentive for eating.

From the moment she had entered this room there was a grow
ing apprehension about the whole evening. Unable to eat an
feeling more edgy by the moment, Martha knew her mood wa
due to more than the fatiguing events of the past few days or th
death of her loved one.

For a while she concentrated on Mary's lovely face and gra
cious manner, but imitating it was a futile gesture. Martha se
tled down on her couch and resigned herself to simply bein
quiet.

It was just as Deborah took Martha's cup to refill it with win
that Martha snapped into alertness and was able to see what ha
been troubling her about this room.

"Ah, besides my being a guest here in my own house, othe
things trouble me about this room," she said to herself, and
trickle of energy ran through her veins.

*This room, this very couch, the food, the servants coming an
going, the pouring of the wine . . . , her thoughts raced. This i
the very place where I have served Jesus and his men. Tonight
am troubled—no, angry—that for all my times of serving Jesus
he did not come when I needed him. How often have I set plate
of food before him, poured wine into his cup, and remove*

mpty dishes from this table for him and his men? she wondered.
he memory, like a sharp needle, picked steadily at her. *Where as he? What had kept him away? Why had he not come?* Over *nd* over the questions surfaced and raised their ugly heads in *er* mind.

The long meal, the first of the traditional thirty days of mourn-*ng,* was friendly but without gaiety. It seemed to drag on end-*essly* like the dry heat of a summer drought.

Once she inwardly admitted her source of anger, Martha ral-*ed* a little. She even managed several polite conversations and a *omewhat* hospitable countenance.

When the final course was served and consumed and the last *uest* spoke his shalom of farewell, Martha heaved a grateful *igh* of relief. They would be back in the morning, but for now *Martha* could mourn privately.

She turned from the street and iron gates, and in the moonlight *he* said to Mary, "Let us go in and help the servants with the *ast* of the cleaning up. Maybe that way we can all go to our *allets* a little earlier tonight."

Without a word Mary moved from the gates, down the *ourtyard,* and into the main doorway. There she stopped, *urned,* and idly looked back out into the empty yard. Gently *Martha* touched her arm, bringing her into the house, and shut *he* massive doors behind her.

"Come," Martha said affectionately. But Mary did not re-*pond.* She stood by the doors, head bowed, toying with the hem *f* her head veil.

Martha looked down intently into Mary's face and questioned, Are you feeling ill, my sister?"

Mary's answer was barely audible, and Martha leaned for-*ard* to hear.

"No, I am not ill. I think I'm just tired, or maybe, to be more *onest,* I am disappointed. I was so sure the Lord would come," *er* voice trailed off into nothing.

Martha felt she was gifted in making the best of every situation *nd* most of her solutions to problems involved doing something; *o* with the old vigor in her tone, she said, "Then, let's help the *ervants.* It will occupy our minds and our hands."

Martha was halfway across the main hall before she realize
Mary had not moved. She stopped, turned around, and wit
low-keyed deliberation in her voice, said sternly, "Mary, I a
not only disappointed about Jesus, I am angry that he did n
come, but it is over. Lazarus is gone. He rests in God's arm
tonight, and I pray he is no longer in pain. We must pick up th
pieces of our lives. Now, come with me, and we will busy ou
selves with the tasks at hand."

Still Mary did not move. She stood leaning against the mai
doors, totally absorbed in her own thoughts.

Martha's well of patience had never been too deep, but at th
moment it ran bone-dry, and sharply she said, "Mary, I hav
gladly taken care of you, Lazarus, and this whole household.
have supervised the spring planting and the summer harvestin
of our fields and vineyards. With Joseph's help I have seen to th
raising of our sheep and other livestock. Very seldom have
asked you to serve, to take part in the housekeeping, or to wor
at some dreary task. It is beyond my comprehension that when
need you—really need you—you withdraw, or worse, you di
appear, leaving me with the whole burden of the tasks at hand
Or, like now, when we both are confused and hurt by Jesu
actions, we should pledge ourselves to tasks. Even simple one
would help to ease our troubled minds."

Martha did not expect or even wait for an answer. She turne
on her heel and headed briskly for the cooking area.

Mary could not see her sister go for the scalding tears whic
were streaming down her face, but still she did not move.

Martha reached the cooking area, and it was dark except fo
the light of one small lamp. The neighbor women and servar
girls had done their work remarkably well. Everyone was gon
and everything, except for one basket, was in its proper place
Even by the light of the small hanging lamp in the corner, Marth
could see that things were in excellent order. She turned aroun
and decided to give the dining room one final check before sh
retired.

When she left the cooking area and padded silently across th
carpets of the main hall to the dining room, Martha knew, befor
she looked, that Mary had gone to her room without bidding he

good night. Martha felt a twinge of guilt for the tartness of her tongue, but she quickly rationalized that it was not the first time Mary had failed to see to the tasks.

Why should I expect anything else? she wondered. *My sister is not given to menial work or serving. Mary is gifted in singing, in needlework and embroidering, in listening and laughing, in just . . . ,* she searched for the elusive word. "Ah, in just being," Martha finished aloud. *I must be more tolerant with her, but she is so different from me.* Martha's thoughts continued until she reached the dining room.

There were no lamps lit so Martha retraced her steps, and taking a small burning lamp from the great hall, returned and lit one of the large lamp stands in the corner.

She stood looking at the long, low table and couches which were all illuminated by the lamp's glow and said to herself, "My sister is like this room with its soft golden look—so alive to life. She is always 'being,' whereas I seem to be always consumed by 'doing.' "

The tabletop shone because of someone's careful polishing, and Martha noticed the large bronze urn was back in its place of honor between the two candelabra.

It was in this room and at this very table, Martha remembered, she had learned firsthand about the vast difference between Mary's creative "being" and her own inescapable urge toward "doing."

One evening, just at sunset, Martha and Mary had washed the feet of Jesus and seven of his men who accompanied him.

Then, taking Jesus by the arm, Martha led him into the house and held a ceremonial robe out for him to wear as the guest of honor.

Both Mary and Martha escorted the group to their places at the table. It was not the first dinner they had taken together, but routinely Martha personally seated Jesus at the couch which was exactly midway in the long table. Each dinner she did that so everyone could see and hear him at the best advantage.

Martha remembered how they all marveled at this man called Jesus from Nazareth.

His looks completely startled her. They certainly caught her

off guard the first time she saw him coming through her gates. It
was as if she had seen him before in a dream or a vision, though
she could not immediately tell why.

He was irresistibly winsome and incredibly handsome of face.
His skin, tanned and golden from the Galilean sun, was unblemished and his short, dark beard framed his symmetrical features with a manly grace.

Jesus' eyes were not the same bright azure blue of Mary's but
were of a softer, paler, grayer blue, given to subtly changing
with his words or moods.

It was weeks after she first met him that Martha suddenly
realized why she felt she had known or seen him before.

Long ago, when she had been memorizing the psalms with
Lazarus, she had pictured in her mind how the beautiful,
"comely" King David would have looked.

Jesus, with his blue gray eyes, noble nose, and superb features, matched her mind's image of David perfectly. It had given
her chills when she finally put it all together.

Everyone was attracted to him. Martha and Mary often discussed and agreed that it was the first glimpse at his fairness of
face which arrested one's attention, but it was definitely his
penetrating way of returning one's look that held and transfixed
one. It was also Mary who first remarked on the faint circles
under his eyes, which gave a look of sorrow to his face in spite of
his comeliness.

Noisy children became quiet around him and shyly crept
close, simply to be near him. Children of soft-spoken natures
took his hand, warmed to him, played little games on his fingers
and spontaneously giggled in noisy delight.

Young people cocked their heads to sharpen their listening
skills so they would not miss anything he said. And no one, old
or young, was immune to his dramatic way of telling a story.

"But always," Martha had remarked to Mary as they were
sewing one day, "there is the way Jesus looks at each person."

"Yes," Mary had answered, "and I could easily lose myself
in that gaze."

Jesus' strong intelligence and straightforward honesty reminded Martha of her father; yet his tenderness and ability to be creative were like the traits she saw and loved in Mary and Lazarus.

Jesus, though tall and slim, was a man of unbending strength. His years at his father's carpenter's bench vigorously wielding the tools of his trade had toughened and strengthened the sinews and muscles of his limbs. But while he was iron strong, he seemed flexible and unhardened.

He seemed stubbornly dedicated to principles; yet he was pliable and tender.

Martha loved his bluntness of speech, the way he never wasted words, and his honest, truthful directness; yet she was touched beyond belief by the utmost kindness which framed all his conversations. He was obviously filled with authority; yet he was human, warm, and touchable. Martha always thought of him as the most whole and healthy man she had ever seen. It seemed to Martha that Jesus, teacher and rabbi, was a most complete man.

When he was in her home, Martha found herself unable to do enough for him. She was skilled in serving, treating, and even healing others; yet his presence in her house inspired her to unbelievable heights of giving and doing. Jesus' slightest gesture or look was met by Martha's immediate consideration, and off she would fly to fulfill his need. She could not put her finger on the exact reason for her desire to serve him, only that it was so. It was as if he had touched a responsive chord deep within her being, and serving him became her most compelling urge.

Whenever word reached her that Jesus was teaching in Jerusalem, she went into a flurry of frenzied activity, for she knew he would come for a visit. It was such a short walk from the temple courtyard in Jerusalem to her front gate that Jesus rarely spent his evening meal or night's lodging any place but in Martha's spacious house. It was an unspoken agreement between them, and it was these visits which deepened the loving friendship between Martha, Mary, Lazarus, and Jesus.

With Jesus' visits, Mary grew pensive and quiet. "It is as if," she told Martha one night as they climbed the steps to the rooftop, "I want to store everything in my heart. I dare not miss a thing he says or does. I have the feeling I will someday wish I had listened more."

Martha smiled in the darkness as they reached the roof, because if Jesus' friendship made Mary quiet and reflective, it did just the opposite to Lazarus and her.

Lazarus, always lethargic from the long debilitating effects of his lingering illness, would become suddenly alive with a restless stirring of life whenever Jesus was near. Martha called Jesus' influence on Lazarus "a medicine which doeth good!"

So it was. Lazarus would find strength from somewhere and energetically begin to question Joseph about the sheep and goats, the barley fields, or worse, he would ask Martha what needed repairing in the house. Once when Jesus was there, Lazarus, in his usual short burst of good health, determined to fix the hinge on a small, priceless wooden cabinet. Jesus watched Lazarus struggling with the delicate bolts for as long as he could, then laughing and shaking his head he said, "Not only are you going to break the hinge even more than it is already, but you are attaching it upside down, and it may never work."

Lazarus picked up the pieces of hinge and the cabinet, and in a voice replying with mock seriousness, he laid it ceremoniously at Jesus' feet saying, "It seems I have forgotten you have earned your master skills in carpentry; so I bow to your abilities." He would have said more, but both men were absorbed in their laughter.

Martha had stood in the doorway quietly observing the deep, loving friendship which was forging together before her eyes. How good it was to hear her brother laugh, to see him try to do things, and to see him so much better, even if it were a temporary time of well-being.

She understood well this burst of enthusiasm for life when Jesus was visiting, because it happened to her as well.

Martha was always seized with pride that this gifted rabbi would make her home his choice, and her hospitality knew no limits. Nothing was too good or ever spared for Jesus and his men. The willingness to serve him was so strong in Martha that it overflowed to each person he had brought with him. She never knew exactly how many people it would be for the evening meal or how many floor mats for sleeping she would lay out; only that never, in the two or three years, did Jesus ever come alone. It was all an incredible challenge to Martha's skill and sense of devotion to duty. She took to it like an experienced eagle soaring into tumultuous, stormy winds.

The dinner she remembered the most was the one with Jesus, his seven men, and five hastily added neighbors. It was not one of the biggest groups she had served, but Naomi was ailing and both Deborah and Leah had been scalded by the boiling soup as they had lifted the pot from the fire; so the work load was lying heavy on Martha's shoulders.

After seating Jesus and serving the first course of cracked-wheat cakes and cucumbers which were dipped in the bowls of oil and vinegar, she had gone back to the cooking area to do what she could about salvaging what was left of the barley soup. To her relief, not much of it was gone although the girls, holding their burned hands in basins of cool water, were sure all the soup had spilled on them.

"Mary?" Martha called, looking past the girls and out to the back court. "Are you out there?"

There was no answer, and Leah ventured, "I think she is with the guests."

"I see," said Martha as she poured the soup into a large bowl and carried it on a tray to the dining room.

When she reached the room, she placed the tray on a small chest by the wall and wiped her hands on a towel as she looked for Mary. Martha almost missed her, because Mary was on the floor between the couches of Jesus and her gladdened brother. When she caught sight of the top of Mary's red hair, she called out, "Mary!" and instantly regretted the ugly impatience in her voice.

Everyone fell silent as if her call had been not one voice but a flourish of trumpet blasts at the temple. Everyone turned to look at her, and some of them hid their smiles as they watched the red stain of embarrassment creep up her neck and spread over her cheeks.

She was definitely obliged to explain; so she stammered, "Ah,

excuse me, friends, honored guest, but . . . ." Then, lookin
directly at Jesus, she lamented, "Master, do you not care tha
my sister just sits here while I do all the work?" She did not wa
for an answer but plunged boldly on, "Tell her to come and hel
me."

If the room had quieted down before, when she had called ou
Mary's name, it now was as if everyone had suddenly stoppe
breathing. Without sound, they waited for Jesus' reply.

No one missed his words or message, thought Martha; *no on
but me,* she remembered sadly. All she could recall of the mo
ment was that there was no look of condemnation on his fac
and no threat in his tone of voice, but his answer mystified an
confused her thoroughly. He said, "Martha, Martha, dea
friend, you are so upset over all these details." He waved hi
hand over the dishes before him. "There is really only one thin
worth being concerned about. Mary has discovered it, and
won't take it away from her!"

The gentle friendship of his spirit reached out and touche
her, but to Martha his frustrating remarks left her with precisel
the same work load plus more questions.

She looked at Jesus, and Mary, still seated beside him
shrugged her shoulders and mutely concentrated on picking u
the vinegar and oil bowls to make room for the barley soup.

Cold soup—by the time I get it served, Martha's thought
pronounced.

Routinely she managed to get all the guests served withou
mishap, until she got to Andrew. There, between the table an
Andrew's couch, Martha's foot caught itself in her robe, throw
ing her off balance, and every drop of lukewarm barley sou
spread itself over Andrew's head and robe. She was horrified a
her clumsiness.

"It's alright, Martha," Andrew said as he jumped up on hi
feet. "In fact, it wasn't hot; so I'm not burned—only wet. See?
He was laughing and making the best of the situation.

Martha groaned inwardly and then mumbled to Andrew
"Come with me. I'll get you a clean tunic!"

They left amid the guests' growing chorus of chuckling an

aughter. No one could recall seeing Martha embarrassed in a
ear's time, much less twice in one evening.

Disgusted by the way the whole day had gone and her cheeks
urning with indignation over her inept hospitality, Martha hur-
ied out ahead of Andrew.

7

THE friendship between Martha and Andrew began when they were much younger.

How strange the pathways of God, Martha thought as she remembered how her family had traveled from Bethany to the distant seaport of Capernaum and had unexpectedly become acquainted with Andrew and Simon.

Even stranger was her meeting up with Andrew after several years of silence, for they seemed to pick up the friendship exactly where they had left it.

When she was just a little girl, Martha recalled, the trip to Capernaum was an exciting, adventuresome one, at least to her thinking. From Bethany they traveled by vast camel caravan northward, the way of the mountain, through the despised country of Samaria, and finally to Capernaum, which was located on the northern edge of the Sea of Galilee.

It was a place of breathtaking beauty. Martha never stopped marveling at the glittering sea shaped like a harp. The lake itself looked like some of the rare jewelry pieces from her father's shop—a bright opal surrounded by precious green emeralds. Everything at the sea of Galilee overflowed with a flood of sunshine. The natural perfume of the balmy air and the turtledove of the surrounding hills and valleys breathed together in an exquisite tribute to Jehovah's creativity.

Once, when Mary was taking in all the beauty, she said "Mother must have been exactly like this place—serene, yet alive and beautiful!" Martha savored the observation each time they visited the enchanting sea.

The noisy seaport of Capernaum was one of the largest towns that circled the lake.

It bustled in a maze of activity, not only because of its large fishing colony, but also because it was a frontier town for the great crossroads from Egypt to Damascus and from Acre to the Far East.

Merchants, including Martha's father, came from distant cities to avail themselves of the rich supply of goods. They filled Capernaum with their clamorous bargaining. Their presence made it an important commercial town, just as hundreds of fishermen made it a flourishing fishing port.

Over the years, many lovely cashmeres, silks, and tapestries had been purchased here by Josiah, and his shop in Jerusalem had earned its reputation for exquisite and unique merchandise because of his buying trips to Capernaum.

However, it was not for commercial reasons that Martha, Mary, and Lazarus made the long, arduous journey.

Josiah had loved Rachel so much, he decided soon after her death that the best way to keep her memory alive was to take Martha, Mary, and even ailing Lazarus to the place of their mother's birth. So they made the pilgrimage to Capernaum once a year or as often as Josiah could arrange the time away from his shop.

Martha and Mary always stood the rather exhausting trip better than their brother. However, once they got to their destination, viewed the shimmering blue Sea of Galilee, and were joyously received by their kinsfolk, everyone forgot the difficult trip. Even Lazarus's color returned to his cheeks, and if he tired or felt ill, it was of little consequence. Nothing, it seemed, spoiled their joy.

The children especially loved their mother's exuberant sister, Miriam. Her quick laugh, together with her dark, dancing eyes, made her a delight to be around, and she lovingly fed the hungering needs of Martha and Mary with her warm, woman-to-woman talks. Privately, Josiah encouraged Miriam to spend as much time with them as she could. He never told her how his own heart fluttered and beat erratically each time he saw so much of Rachel's reflection in her.

Twice Miriam had miscarried, but instead of becoming hardened and embittered about her barrenness, she opened her hea... to everyone else's children. It was natural then that her love f... Rachel's three could not be contained; so it spilled out of her as ... many splendored waterfall. It was also no wonder that the... loved her in return.

Miriam's fisherman husband, their Uncle Judah, was cut fro... a different cloth, but once the children discovered the warm... giving heart he concealed by a stern countenance and a dee... voice, they fell to loving him as well.

While Mary was busily learning some new embroidery stitc... from Aunt Miriam and Lazarus was over at the synagogue listen... ing to Capernaum's rabbi, Martha was usually down on th... beach busily being Judah's shadow. Doggedly she followed him... helped with the nets occasionally, and once or twice actuall... sailed with him.

During one visit, when Martha had been about twelve years o... age, she begged, pleaded, and cajoled her uncle to take her wit... him in his large fishing boat. Finally he gave in.

"Enough of this pleading, child! I do have a small bit of busi... ness with Jonas who fishes out of Bethsaida. So, instead o... walking over there, we will go by boat. Will that suffice you?... He playfully tapped the top of her head.

Even though Martha knew the trip would be very short, sinc... Bethsaida was the neighboring town just east of Capernaum, sh... fairly shouted, "Oh, yes, Uncle Judah, that would be ver... good!" Then in case he changed his mind about sailing with ... girl, she gathered up her skirt and waded out into the wate... toward the boat as fast as she could go.

There were large colonies of fishermen all along the edge o... the great sea, and on that particular sunny, cloudless day as the... sailed to Bethsaida, Martha breathed in the fresh, damp sea air... let the sun wash her face with warmth, and listened attentivel... to all the calling and friendly greetings shouted back and fort... between Judah and the men in the passing boats.

It was also on that day, after they arrived at Bethsaida, tha... Martha first saw and met Jonas and his two young sons.

It was not that she would have missed them—what with her uncle pointing them out as he admonished, "Mark my words, Martha child, those sons of Jonas will be the best fishermen in all of this great sea one day. They, like their father, are shrewd about the fickle ways of the water, and they have a God-given natural talent for knowing where the fish spend their mornings."

Judah threw a rope to one of the boys, and the young man deftly caught it, pulled it in, and beached the boat on the hard, white sand.

Clearly, when her uncle was with his fishing friends, he was transformed from the quiet, almost grave man she knew to an outspoken man in familiar territory. Martha watched him in amazement.

Between gaily shouted greetings and humorous remarks with other fishermen, Judah said to Jonas and his sons, "This is one of Miriam's kinsfolk from the south, and her name is Martha."

Noting that she was a girl, the taller of the two sons teased, "Does she sail well, Judah?"

"Well, considering it took us many long days on this voyage, yes, I'd say she sails surprisingly well," he winked at the boy as he exaggerated their trip.

Then to Martha he said good-naturedly, "This is Simon, the oldest. Do not mind his flapping mouth. Simon is like this sea," Judah said pointing toward the rippling water, "with a capricious temperament all his own."

She was clutching up her skirts when Simon rather awkwardly helped her from the boat. More accurately, he jerked her out, but Martha was impressed by his strength. He was very tall, rawboned, and trim. He was bare from the waist up, and she could see the muscles under the skin of his wet arms and shoulders rippling in the glistening sunlight.

She understood her uncle's admiration for the boys, because even though she was just meeting them, she could clearly see Simon's physical strength, and she liked the way he took charge of things.

". . . and this is Simon's brother, Andrew," Judah was saying.

Martha turned and looked up directly into the second boy's brown eyes. He smiled, and so did she, but neither of them said anything.

Martha liked him better than his brother, though she could not tell why.

Andrew was not quite as tall as Simon but built as slim and with the same powerful chest and arms. Both boys had a head of hair a few shades darker red than Mary's, and while neither of them could be considered handsome, Martha had to admit they were striking and bore watching.

Toward the end of their visits to Capernaum, before their father's death, Martha, Mary, and Lazarus all enjoyed and deepened their friendship with Andrew and Simon. Martha never warmed completely to Simon's teasing and "flapping mouth," and during the first summer she grew to know him, she learned to move out of his way quickly when things went wrong. His temper was instantaneous and the heated oaths he bellowed were known to scorch people's ears. "Simon's voice can be ear rending!" Martha had warned Mary.

But his dedication to fishing was obvious, and because of his skill, he drew the admiration of the other fishermen. Simon, she agreed with her Uncle Judah, was a young man to reckon with even if he was not to her liking.

With Andrew it was a different story. At first he said almost nothing directly to Martha, but later they slipped into a quiet casual relationship, for they found they could be friends with just a few words spoken between them. It was Andrew who recognized Martha's skilled and agile fingers one day as he watched her at Miriam's weaving loom. So, without much talk between them, he set about to teach her the fisherman's ancient art of mending torn nets. She proved an apt pupil and became almost as fast as he was. Their unique friendship solidified near the nets and the barrels of salted fish on the warm, sunny edge of the sea.

The family stopped going to Capernaum after the deaths of their father and Martha's husband, Benjamin, and except for news passed from one caravan to another, Martha lost track of Jonas's sons of Bethsaida.

She was stunned one day to learn from a trader that Andrew, from all reports, had left Bethsaida and had gone off to follow the strange, new prophet named John. For no particular reason, she wondered if Andrew had married and then answered her own question by remembering he was a good Jew, even devout, and so naturally he would have taken a wife by now.

But Andrew was so good at fishing and preserving the fish with salt that Martha could not imagine him away from his boats, nets, and his beloved sea. Yet, apparently the wild man from the desert had been most impressive.

Then three winters ago, while she was sitting at her loom weaving some flax into linen cloth, Mary had burst in the room saying, "Come look who is at our front gate, Martha. You'll not believe it!" and without saying anything else Mary turned and flew out the doorway like a darting sparrow.

Martha got up quickly and almost knocked over her loom. Running closely after Mary, both women reached the gate and heard the man quietly ask, "May I come in, old friends?"

"Andrew! Is it really you?" Martha asked, shading her eyes from the sunlight and searching his face intently.

"Yes, Martha, it is I. Now, may I come in?"

"Oh, forgive me," Martha cried, and hurriedly she and Mary pulled open the gate. They went inside amid the confusion of them asking questions of him.

"Wait!" shouted Martha, holding her hand up to get their attention. "Let's get Lazarus down here, and after we have eaten something and you have caught your breath, then we can all calmly ask questions, and you can answer."

She looked up at Andrew, and then stepped over closer to him for a better look.

"You must be weary, and you've probably not eaten today." He nodded, and they knew what she had said was true.

However, barely after they started to eat dinner, they could hold their questions no longer; so Lazarus began. He asked of Andrew's father, Jonas.

"He is dead," Andrew answered simply.

"So is ours," echoed back Lazarus. The room grew momentarily hushed.

"What of Simon?" asked Mary, hoping the conversation would lighten.

"Ah, that is why I've come. I want to tell you about Simon." He hesitated ever so slightly, and Mary looked intently across the table to read his face better.

"Well, what I want to know," interrupted Martha as she rushed in with a forgotten tray of dried figs, "is not about Simon. I want to know about the rumor we heard of your running off with a prophet! Surely this is not true!"

"Dear outspoken Martha," said Andrew, chuckling softly. "I am not with John now," he said.

"Ah," said Martha knowingly. "When I heard you had gone with him, I knew it would not be for long. You are too good a fisherman to leave your work." Rushing on, she confidently continued. "Then, too, the sons of Jonas have built quite a name for themselves in the fishing colony up there, and I just knew you couldn't leave it forever," she finished, proud of her accuracy.

"That's just it, though. It's what I want to tell you all. I have left my fishing; so has Simon. We do not fish for fish anymore . . . ." He stopped talking to let the words sink in.

Then he continued. "My leaving the fishing nets is only one of a great many changes I have experienced recently." His voice grew husky, and for a moment he cleared his throat noisily.

"Even the man I followed is gone. John the Baptist was arrested by Herod Antipas, imprisoned in the underground vaults, and . . . ." Andrew bowed his head until he was able to go on. "He died a hideous death, one I cannot yet speak of . . . ."

Down went his head, so they would not view the depths of his anguish.

They sat stiff and silent around the table until Mary roused herself and, leaning over, touched Andrew's arm, saying, "Tell us then, Andrew, from the beginning, so we may understand."

"I would like to very much." Andrew's voice softened and filled with a comfortable love. "But I am not sure you will understand. Some of this I do not understand myself, but the old bonds of friendship run deep between us, so I know at least you will listen. I pray you will see what I'm doing is what I must."

"Proceed, please," Martha urged.

"I hesitate to begin it, because when I left Bethsaida to follow John, it seemed such an accidental thing. Yet what it led to was not a chance happening or a whim of fate.

"Everyone in Bethsaida and Capernaum talked about the teachings and prophesying of this man called John. When I found he was preaching down by the city of Magdala, I thought I'd go and see the man for myself.

"So another fisherman, John, the son of Zebedee, and I went to see this man they called John the Baptist."

"We have heard of him, too," put in Mary, "and he sounded so strange . . . living in the desert . . . ."

"Eating locusts and wild honey. Is that true, Andrew?" Martha, always concerned with what to serve for dinner, needed to know.

"Yes, it is true. But when I saw him for myself, I cannot tell you how deeply he stirred my soul."

"Was he not wild then?" Martha asked, but Lazarus's glance silenced her.

Andrew continued. "He was like no man we have ever seen—bursting with rugged health, strong, and intense of vision. He was impetuous and full of fire. I thought of him as a young Elijah, ready to penetrate the people's hearts and minds with his incredible message. Why he was put to death and by what evil intentions burns in my soul even now."

Martha marveled at Andrew's way with words. Whatever this prophet John had done, at least he had loosened Andrew's tongue, and his words streamed eloquently on. She listened intently now.

"The prophet had a special kind of grace about him. You could see it in his humility and his holylike courage. His self-denial and abstinence were so great, many people thought him possessed and said, 'He has a devil in him.' But my friend John and I wanted to know him better."

"You did not think him, at least, strange?" questioned Lazarus gently.

"At first we did, but then we listened to his words. I confess, when he prophesied about the man who was to come, we believed him. It did not matter that John looked strange or lived in a way different from mine. We both felt the man spoke the truth and spoke it as no other man ever had.''

Eventually the lamps were lit, and they eagerly lingered around the table listening to Andrew as he told of how John and he had left their fishing to go off with John the Baptist to be his followers.

"I intended to return to fishing after a few weeks or months of serving with the prophet, but somehow, as the work grew, I continued on.''

"We, in Bethany, heard that this John the Baptist predicted the Messiah's return. Is this what you believe?'' Martha asked, her mind spinning with thoughts, trying to recall her religious classes with Lazarus and the rabbi.

"Yes, and I especially believed the prophet one day in the other village of Bethany, you know, the one across the Jordan River?'' They nodded their heads in accord.

"Well,'' Andrew leaned forward as he spoke, "I believed it because as John was baptizing some people in the river, he suddenly stopped and pointed to a man who was walking down the hill through the trees toward the riverbank.

"John seemed to be transfixed in the water. Then, as he pointed to the man, he cried out, 'Behold the Lamb of God!' He proceeded to tell everyone this man would take away the sins of the world. His voice was blazing with the fire of knowledge and authority.

"I was standing close to the water's edge when the man waded into the water right in front of me. For a moment he looked at me, and I stood face to face with the man they call Jesus the Nazarene.

"Then John baptized him.''

"Did you speak to this Jesus?'' Mary asked intently.

"No, not then, for my courage failed me. But the next day while my friend John, Zebedee's son, and I were talking with John the Baptist, Jesus walked through the small group of people gathered to hear the prophet, and the same thing happened.

"John turned and again, in a loud voice, declared, 'There is he Lamb of God' as he pointed to Jesus.

"I cannot explain it," continued Andrew, shaking his head, as f to clear it, "but at that moment both John and I knew we would leave John the Baptist and become Jesus' followers in- stead.

"We watched Jesus walk away after John had pointed him out again, and while we did not know where he was going, we pur- ued him anyway.

"Jesus must have known we were behind him, because pres- ntly he turned and asked quietly but directly what we wanted.

"Neither of us knew precisely, and we were both timid in his awesome presence. But we wanted to be with him; so we asked vhere he was staying. He bid us come, and we went with him. 'or several hours we just sat listening."

"Whose house was he staying in?" Martha questioned.

"No one's," he answered. "It was just a temporary booth, ike the common people put up, with sides made of woven green branches of terebinth and palm and the top covered with a triped cloth. But to us, because he was there, it seemed the perfect place to be.

"I tell you," here Andrew leaned toward them, his eyes blaz- ng with a fiery dedication, "before John and I closed our eyes hat night, we felt in our innermost hearts, because of what we had heard that afternoon, that the Kingdom of Heaven had come. We felt we had been in the presence of him who was a priest greater than Aaron, a prophet greater than Moses, and a king greater than David!"

"Andrew," Martha's voice exclaimed, "from our childhood I remember you as reticent to utter three words together at one ime; yet here you are speaking to us as we have rarely heard anyone speak. You are so changed!" Martha's words summed up Lazarus's and Mary's thoughts completely.

"I am unaware of my speech changes, Martha," Andrew said as he smiled broadly. "But you are right about my changing. I m changed, and it all happened once I'd seen the Nazarene.

"In fact, John and I were both so changed by Jesus that the very next day, at John the Baptist's urging, we decided to leave the Baptist and learn everything we could from Jesus.

"We left the Jordan River and returned to Bethsaida to te Simon and our kinsfolk of our decisions. I was bursting to te Simon that we had found the promised Messiah!"

"Then, you believe this Jesus might indeed be the lon awaited King?" Lazarus asked, his voice cracking with a tonishment.

"No, not might be—*is* the King!" Andrew thundered.

Martha spoke. "Ah, I would imagine, knowing Simon, that h would have none of your story."

"That's exactly right, Martha. There I was, full of the e thusiasm of a zealot since I had just been face to face with th true, living Messiah, and Simon, who had been into the win skins a little too much, just yelled, 'Get into the boat. We've g a lot of fishing to make up because of your religious wande ing.' "

"With Simon's tongue, I'm sure he said a lot more than that muttered Martha, just under her breath.

"Andrew, please continue," Mary said, dismissing Martha quip.

"Well, there was nothing I could do but go with my brothe Simon to the boats. He is persuasive, that one. All the time w sat in the boat mending the nets, I told him about the prophe John, the baptizing at the Jordan, and my time with Jesus, bu Simon just worked fast and furiously on the nets. He called me madman, among other things.

"Then, while we were still mending the nets, arguing an shouting at one another, someone called out to us. We bot looked up, and to my surprise I recognized Jesus. He cupped hi hand to his mouth and called out, 'Come along with me, and will show you how to fish for the souls of men!' Simon stared Jesus and his great mouth dropped open and stayed that way.

"Jesus' voice was sure and strong. It had an almost musica quality to it, but clearly it was a commanding clarion call. Yet was warm with joy. Even now shivers run down my back wit just the remembering!

"What struck me the most about Jesus' voice was the certai sound of hope. Oh, how good it rang in my ears and in the depth f my soul. It was a sound I've longed to hear all my life. Think f it—hope in these ugly times."

Andrew grew distant for a moment, and with the memory his ace softened in the lamplight.

Then he picked up his story, "All the fishermen in the boats hat day and the children playing on the shore heard the call of esus. Yet, it was almost funny, for it was my brother Simon, vho, without my identifying Jesus, dropped his nets as if they vere a handful of poisonous snakes and immediately leaped over he boat's edge. He landed in the water, waded to shore, and ran ver to Jesus without a question.

"I had to run to catch up with him. I could see Jesus laughing nd shaking his head at Simon's impetuousness. But when we inally stood before him, Jesus' eyes and face sobered, and he ooked deep into our souls with his royal gaze. I felt he read, ntuitively, our innermost thoughts. Then he looked intently at Simon. It was as if, in just a glance, he could see the man before im as a fisherman, good at his trade but with certain flaws and veaknesses; yet he seemed to see something in Simon we had never seen. Jesus and Simon stared at each other, their eyes ocked together in an intense soul-searching confrontation. When he finally spoke, Jesus said with great authority, 'You are Simon, Jonas's son, but from now on you shall be called Peter, he rock.' Simon, though he was a head taller than Jesus, seemed to shrink in size under Jesus' quiet pronouncement.

"We left our boats, our nets, our families, and our livelihood. We cut them out as quickly as if we were cleaning a fish with a sharp knife.

"I had never done anything so extraordinary or so decisive before. For some time after, I found it hard to draw my breath, and my heart pounded within me at what we had done!"

Then Lazarus asked, "You have left a wife and perhaps sons and daughters?" No one noticed that Martha's shoulders straightened or that she ever so slightly leaned forward.

"No, I have not married." Martha's mouth relaxed, and a tiny smile appeared.

"Peter is married, and our leaving created quite a furor. He said he would be back, but Anna, his wife, and Sarah, his

mother-in-law, wagered that he'd never return. There was ba
blood between them, and I left Capernaum relieved that I ha
not yet found a helpmate.''

"Still, you picked up and left everything?" asked Lazarus.

"Yes, my friend, because then, as now, I believed John th
Baptist's testimony and his prophetic words, and I believ
Jesus, the man, himself. I could do nothing but give myself t
him.''

"What else happened the day you left your nets?" Mary wa
eager to hear all.

Andrew turned to her. "Let's see," he said, rubbing his eye
"We walked up the beach a little farther, and though the shore
were crowded with men, children, boats, and fishing tools, Jesu
went directly to the boats of Zebedee. The old man oversees a
the exporting of salt-packed fish, and he and his sons are ver
wealthy because of their trade skills. Zebedee's two sons wer
repairing some wooden kegs when Jesus came toward them an
greeted John whom he had met when we were with John th
Baptist. Then he looked at the other son, James, and said quit
simply, 'James and John, follow me.'

"I thought old Zebedee's eyes would burst and fall out of h
head, because both his sons turned from Jesus and, facing the
father, thanked him courteously for their home and their lovin
memories. Then they embraced him warmly and said the
farewells, leaving Zebedee wild-eyed and ranting with angr
questions about who would run their exporting business.''

"Zebedee *is* the most successful fisherman in all Galilee, an
his success is due in part to his skilled sons. You mean the
climbed out of the boat, just like that?" Martha was incredulou
her face a mask of questioning frowns.

"Yes, just like the rest of us," Andrew answered.

"How many more are there of 'you'?" Lazarus wanted t
know.

"Besides Peter and myself, there're Zebedee's sons, Jame
and John; another fisherman, Philip; and his friend, Nathanae
But not all have left their nets. One was a tax collector, anothe
was a revolutionary, and there are several more.''

"Andrew!" Martha's astounded shout split the air. "Yo

ean you are with a group of men, disciples if you please, and
ne of them is a tax collector?"

Andrew cleared his throat. "I said he *was* a tax collector. His
ame is now Matthew, but you may remember him as Levi."

"Not Levi, the tax collector from Capernaum?"

"Yes, the same," Andrew answered matter-of-factly.

"But," now Martha was sputtering, "but he is the worst tax
coundrel anywhere. You know he worked hand in glove with
he Romans. I remember my father's hatred for him, and he
poke of Levi as a traitor!" Rushing on, she continued, "Then
here's the tax collectors' greedy practice of squeezing out a
rofit for themselves over and above what the Romans demand.
evi, more than all his evil henchmen, sucked the blood of de-
ent hardworking people. Moreover," and now her words were
calding, but her voice was low and filled with contemptuous
corn, "he collects taxes from prostitutes, and I'm sure he and
ther collectors take their money out in trade.

"They are not decent men but unclean and to be with one,
uch less Levi or Matthew or whatever he is called now, ren-
ers *you* unclean!"

"Martha," Andrew said wearily, "I told you he *was* a tax
ollector. He is not one now. Matthew has left his collection
oxes, his hoard of silver shekels, and even his two slaves who
rotected him. He is a disciple of Jesus now, as I am. He has put
is old life behind him."

"Like you left fishing?" Mary understood.

"Yes. Like I left fishing," he nodded.

Then, as if Martha should know the rest as well, he said to her,
"There's more. We even ate in Levi's house. Jesus, Peter,
ames, John, and I. Present also were men of dubious, possibly
riminal, professions, and women of obvious ill repute."

Martha gasped and then glared at him. Mary sat in total since, not daring to believe what she heard.

Finally Martha collected herself to ask, "Whose idea was it
. . to eat with him?"

"Jesus'." Andrew got up from the couch and table and slowly
aced the room. "You see, Jesus has come to redeem us, to
ather his chosen people."

Martha could sense his desperate sincerity; so she made
willful effort to understand.

Andrew continued, "I know it is hard to grasp, but Jesus ha
come for sinners, obnoxious publicans, Samaritans, and poss
bly even the Romans."

The two sisters pulled back in genuine horror; so he said, "It
true. Once Jesus said, 'If *anyone* wants to be a follower of min
let him deny himself and take up his cross and follow me.' H
did not say only 'devout, pious Jews' but clearly told us *any* ma
could follow him.

"Martha," and now Andrew sat down across the table fro
her, "Jesus has even taught us that the saying 'Love you
friends and hate your enemies' is wrong. He told us to *love* ou
enemies and to do good to anyone who hates us."

"Even tax men and Romans?" queried Lazarus.

"Yes, we are to pray for those who despitefully use us an
especially those who persecute us."

"It is a hard lesson to learn, and most of us will be unteach
able." Martha spoke harshly.

"I agree, my friend," Andrew said patting Martha's arm in
tender gesture, "but even so, I believe Jesus of Nazareth, th
carpenter's son, is the one foretold by past and present prophet
to be our Deliverer.

"I admit he and his teachings puzzle me, but over and ove
again my heart confirms deep inside of me that he is who he say
he is."

Andrew's voice grew tight with excitement as he talked on. "
tell you, this Jesus, this humble man, is the true Messiah, th
Saviour of the world. I am not merely a follower, but
student—no, a disciple—and I am to be part of his kingdom."

"His kingdom?" they chorused together.

"He is setting up his kingdom?" Mary asked.

"If he is *setting up a kingdom* in Jerusalem, or any place in a
of Judea, he will need several legions of armed men to overthro
the Romans!" said Martha, her mind functioning in its usual
practical manner.

"How many disciples like you are there in all, Andrew?"
Martha pressed.

He answered quietly. "Only twelve, but while I know it does not sound like much, I know we will add to our numbers soon. Why, even now, there are growing numbers of believers, and each day the Master's miracles and fame increase."

"But to set up a kingdom . . . ," Martha's voice trailed off. Then she said matter-of-factly, "From what you told us, Andrew, about this Jesus, if he truly is the awaited Messiah, he will have to do a very thorough job of organizing his plans and recruiting men for his kingdom and cause, or the Romans will crush him and put an end to him before he even gets started. In fact, if he keeps doing things, like eating with men and women of unsavory reputations, he will get into all kinds of trouble. He sounds to me like a man who continually does things he's not supposed to do and says things he's not supposed to say."

All but Andrew nodded their heads in agreement.

From twilight to darkest night and on into the early hours of the dawn, they carried their strange conversation, but for Josiah Ben Jochanan's son and two daughters, the stories of Jesus were to forever alter their lives.

Only a few days later Andrew appeared at their gate again, and Martha, ever hospitable, bid him to come inside.

"No, my dear Martha, not right now, for I must hurry back to the others, but I want you to meet Jesus for yourself.

"He is teaching in the temple. Could I impose on you for the evening meal and tonight's lodging?" Andrew asked. Martha, afraid of offending Andrew, had hesitated only momentarily before answering yes.

The request was only for one evening's meal and one night's lodging, but in the years that followed, the one meal stretched into many, and the one night's lodging became an accepted routine procedure.

Up until the time she met Jesus, she had never quite known what to do with her magnificent house on the hill, but at their first meeting she not only abandoned her preconceived notions about him but caught an extraordinary vision of what her home could do for him.

From the first moment she saw Jesus standing at her front gate with Andrew and the others, she secretly dedicated her house as a place for teaching, resting, and certainly providing food and refreshment for him. It was exactly as Simon had simply climbed out of the boat, leaving his former life behind to follow Jesus. Her decision was impulsive, made without too much thought, but something greater than herself impelled her, and she knew she would make her house—his house.

Martha scrutinized Jesus with a careful eye and marveled as she came towards him that he was dressed in the common, ordinary way of men.

To protect himself from the searing heat of the sun, he wore the simple white kaffiyeh covering his hair. It was fastened in the usual way by an agal around the top of his head.

She warmed to Jesus' humility when she saw he did not wear the white ephod of the Levite or the rich sweeping robes of the scribes, but the long simple blue tallith. It covered his entire person and showed only occasional glimpses of the coarse woolen tunic of striped design and waist girdle underneath.

Nor did he wear on his arm and forehead the tefillin which the Pharisees made so broad. In fact, even the blue ribbon and fringe at the hem of his tallith, which the law required, was not wide or paraded about to show prideful religious obedience. It simply ran the hem of his garment like the fine, discreet line of understated royalty.

Even his leather sandals are like everyone else's, Martha thought, as Jesus came through the entrance gates.

It flashed through her mind that his simple garments did not disguise him. Definitely, Jesus was a king.

As if to confirm her feelings, she watched him and realized Jesus' walk verified his majesty, for he moved, not with a self-appointed haughtiness, but with a natural nobleness and with a distinct touch of grace.

Over the seasons and the years, Martha had tried to describe his facial features, but each attempt ended futilely. No one, it seemed, could draw the same picture. He was to everyone, a different countenance.

It was finally John who gave the most accurate portrait of his face when he said, years later, ". . . the Word became man and lived for a time among us, and we viewed His glory."

The night of the dinner party when she had shouted Mary's name, heard Jesus' puzzling comments, and spilled barley soup over Andrew, Martha had been more tired than she admitted.

As she rushed ahead of Andrew to fetch a clean tunic, she muttered to herself about her habit of overworking herself beyond her limits. *It does so impair my judgment,* she scolded herself.

Andrew's long-legged strides kept up with her hurried trot, but when they reached the cooking area, he grabbed her arm and said, "In the name of hospitality and my good health, wait, Martha, wait!"

"Oh, Andrew, I try so hard, and yet I seem to have no wisdom at all. At least I do not seem to understand the Master sometimes. He speaks in riddles and stories always." She rummaged through a large cupboard for a clean tunic.

"I'm sorry I blurted out Mary's name and asked Jesus to tell her to help me, but it does no good at all if I ask her."

She found the right robe and handed it to Andrew. He caught her hand with the robe, held it steady, and said, "I know, Martha, and I do understand."

She quieted under his gaze and softly, as she looked up at Andrew, she questioned, "Is he displeased with me for doing the thing I do best—serving? It is the only thing I can give to him. Is it wrong to serve, or to need help and seek Mary to share the work load? Oh, I wish I knew."

"Dear Martha, Jesus was not reproving you. At least, if it were a reproof, it was the gentlest, most tender one I've ever heard. No, nor was he scolding you. I feel his words did not demean the work you undertook in his behalf; only he wanted you to put down your anxious spirit of fretting and fussing."

"But, Andrew, we cannot all take our leave of work. Who would feed all those men out there? And how could we all sit in composure at his feet like Mary?"

"Martha, when have you ever sat at his feet?"

Andrew's words stunned her mind as if she had just stepped into the cold, icy stream of water in the creek bed in the uplands.

"I, I have never taken the time. There always seems to be so much to do," she stammered.

She was rubbing her eyes when she heard, "That is the e
sence of what I meant, Martha." She whirled around to lo
directly into the face of Jesus.

His physical presence in the cooking area astounded her. S
stared at him as he continued.

He was smiling and seemed completely at ease among t
trays of food, baskets, and cooking ware. When Jesus spok
Martha was captured by the soothing, gracious warmth of I
words. "Martha, you have always served me and many othe
with an eager openheartedness. Never have you failed anyone
doing things, but you have lost your fine sense of prioritie
You've become overtired, fretful; so much so that serving a
doing have consumed you and taken their toll of you."

He took her chin in his hands, and the small gentle act b
Martha's tears to fill her eyes.

"Martha, Martha," he said as Andrew stood watching,
want to see a balance between *doing* and *being* in your life. Y
need to learn when it is time to stop your industrious serving a
quiet yourself for listening and storing food for your soul. D
you know that the soul must be fed its supper too?"

As he stood before her, Martha's mind was filled with t
portion of a psalm she learned so long ago. The words splash
across her soul like the first refreshing rain of spring:

> Be still, and know that I am God.
> I am exalted among the nations,
> I am exalted in the earth!

Ah, Martha said to herself, *being still is what Mary chose. T
"being" is the better part of "doing." How could I have been
caught up in the serving—the doing?* she puzzled.

"Master," she said, "I shall not forget this moment."

"Nor I," he said simply.

Then after he had looked at her for a moment more, he to
one finger and carefully wiped away the streams of tears on I
cheeks.

There and then, amid the earthy smells of leeks, garlic, a
crusty roasted lamb, both Martha and Andrew felt the h

ajesty of his presence as it slowly filled the room with its agrance of unlimited love and awesome beauty. They grew ent with the wonder of it all. They were so overcome with his lendor that they were never able to speak of the moment ereafter.

8

THE question was never: "Will he die?" It was alway[s]
"When?"

Lazarus was dead now four days, Martha pondered her da[rk]
thoughts as she climbed the stairs to look into his vaca[nt]
chamber. She stood resting her head against the doorpost a[nd]
wondered how it went with the dead after four days. Not findi[ng]
an answer, she sighed and started downstairs to take her mo[rn]-
ing meal.

She tried valiantly to ignore the tentacles of grief whi[ch]
squeezed her bones in painful spasms. She found that by sw[al]-
lowing hard, straightening up her shoulders, and carrying h[er]
head high, she could give at least the appearance of wholene[ss.]
Slowly she walked down the steps, across the main chamb[er]
and opened the front doors.

They saw her just moments before she saw them. The mour[n]-
ers had gathered earlier and were quietly assembled by the ou[ter]
gates, just talking and waiting.

Martha hailed them, briskly walked through the courtya[rd]
gardens, and bid them a somewhat delayed welcome.

Word of Lazarus's death had spread unusually fast[.]
Jerusalem was within easy walking distance. Even thou[gh]
Martha's father was gone, Josiah's wealth and business abiliti[es]
were known and remembered by many. The death, funeral, a[nd]
time of mourning for Josiah's only son attracted a large co[n]-
course of distinguished Jews, and Martha took note of them
with some satisfaction.

They came now in great numbers and waited patiently to [be]
received by the sisters. Some came in loving sadness, others o[ut]

f curiosity, but many came out of their time-honored loyalty to
osiah and the customs of solace.

As Martha walked back into the house with the day's first
nourners, she ran into Mary and exchanged good mornings.

"Have you eaten?" Martha mouthed the words silently to-
vard Mary over the head of Simon, their neighbor.

"Yes. I awakened early. You go get something. I'll stay here
vith the guests." Mary gestured her head towards the cooking
rea.

Martha gave a grateful smile to Mary, excused herself from
he guests, and hurriedly left them to her sister's gracious hospi-
ality.

Even before Martha reached the door, Mary had engaged
nany of them in conversation. *That sister of mine could charm a
narble statue into carrying on a pleasant conversation,* she
hought, and a quick smile flashed across Martha's face.

In the cooking room Naomi was adding her finishing touches
o her hearty corn porridge. She was bending over the pot, gin-
erly tasting the steaming mixture to see if the salt and water
ortions were correct and up to her rigid requirements.

"Is it fit?" Martha winked at Naomi in an attempt to be
umorous and gave the old woman a quick pat on her shoulders.

Naomi had been deep in thought, and Martha's words startled
er, but she recovered quickly and retorted, "Certainly! Would
be any other way?"

The two women's eyes met, but all the fun and pretense fell
way, and the sadness which both women were enduring surged
etween them.

"I know, dear Naomi. We all shall miss Lazarus. It does not
eem right that such a gentle man is gone, but . . . he is."

Words about him were impossible for Naomi; so she bustled
bout and with considerable effort returned to teasing and said,
"Now, if my porridge is not to your satisfaction, I have some
omegranates and dried dates which might suit you better." She
idled out the hot porridge into a deep pottery cup, and the
orners of her mouth turned up into a pleasant smile, but her
yes were red rimmed and damp.

The food refreshed Martha as the fresh morning air had ear-

lier, and she relaxed as she sat on a low stool, eating and talki
with Naomi.

With a good night's rest behind her to clear out the cobwe
from her mind, she realized she had taken the work of Nao
and the others for granted in the past weeks.

"Naomi," Martha said quietly, "I have been so preoccupi
with the events of the past few days and so weary with m
brother's illness, I fear I have neglected you. I want you to kno
I am grateful for your loyalty and your willingness to serve, de
friend."

Naomi made a clucking sound with her tongue and sai
"There's no need for you to fear you have offended me." Sl
gave Martha a loving hug. "I know you see everything, for yo
eyes are everywhere; so you are aware of the fruits of o
labors. Your gratitude, my child, has always quietly shone like
constantly well-filled oil lamp."

The old woman's comment wrapped itself snugly arour
Martha's inner coldness, and she savored its momenta
warmth.

She continued to sit and chat with Naomi and was just finis
ing the last of the porridge and picking at some tiny red pom
granate seeds when she heard Joseph calling her name and the
saw him as he came looking for her.

"What is it, Joseph?" Martha got up and peered at him.

"He is here! I don't mean here. I mean in the grove-garde
down the hill." Joseph's face was wet with running, and h
uneven breathing verified his run.

"Slow down," Martha cautioned. "Now, tell me *who*
here?"

"The Master, Jesus, and most of his disciples," he panted

She snapped to alertness, her eyes alive and wide with a
prehension.

"What is he . . . ?"

"It is true. He waits down there for you, Mistress Martha.
Joseph shouted.

Hurriedly she said to Naomi and Joseph, "Tell no one h
whereabouts. He must have his reasons for staying in the grov
Perhaps his enemies have followed him . . . ."

Martha did not finish her line of thought, nor did she have to tell them where she was going. Instantly she pulled her veil up and over her head. She disappeared out the back doorway, around the side of the house, and slipped through a small opening in the high outer wall which led to a narrow side street.

Downhill she raced, wishing with every footfall she had Tabtha's youth and gazellelike, graceful speed.

Finally she reached the break in the grove's stone wall and entered the grove-garden, ducking and pushing aside the low branches of the olive trees.

Suddenly, as if out of nowhere, someone caught her arm. She stumbled but was immediately pulled up by a sure, firm grip.

"Andrew!" she gasped. "You frightened several years' growth out of me."

What she had wanted to say, but her tongue for once failed her, was that her heart had quickened, not in fearful surprise, but with warm recognition at the sight of him. She was marvelously flooded with gladness at seeing her tall, red-haired friend. She wanted to tell him how right it was that he be in Bethany; how she had missed his quiet, eloquent voice; how she, had she dared, wished he had been with her during the past four days of sorrow.

Instead she determinedly swallowed all her feelings, dismissing them as if they were much too unlikely, and regained her composure to ask, "Now, where is the Master?"

Andrew did not loosen his grip on her arm but began to guide her around flower beds and past leafy trees. As they scrambled through the grove, he said in a low voice, "Jesus' enemies are resourceful, clever, and extremely dangerous. Every day groups of evil men who hate him increase their numbers. They multiply more rapidly than the holes in my fishing nets. It is wise to exercise caution when we travel; so he thought it best to seek refuge here before we ventured up the street to your house."

"Of course," Martha answered simply. Lazarus's care had taken up so much of her time and thoughts that, here again, like forgetting to express her gratitude to Naomi, Martha had forgotten the frightening turn of events for Jesus. She shook her head as if to clear it.

Andrew's calm words and explanation revived her mind, an
she wondered with sharpness if the death noose of Caiaphas, th
high priest, and other religious men of importance would actu
ally tighten around the throat of her friend Jesus.

In remembering Jesus' precarious situation, she also remem
bered her own keen disappointment in his seemingly thoughtles
delay. Perhaps his personal safety was his reason for stayin
away, but Martha couldn't put too much of it all together.

Nor did she have a chance, because at that moment Andre
and she came upon Jesus and his men. They were talking in lo
voices as they sat together on a small, grassy knoll.

With one hand Martha held a tree branch out of her way an
with the other hand on her hip, she looked down at him. She ha
wanted to give him greetings and to be hospitable with th
others, but four days of grieving and four days of questioning le
a bitter-tasting film on her tongue, and she spit out the word
before she could stop herself. "Oh, Lord, if you had been here
my brother would not have died!"

In the hour just before Lazarus's death, Martha had been fille
to overflowing with an abundance of faith. She was so sure o
Jesus' ability to heal, so trusting in his deep friendship, so sur
that he would drop everything to rush to them, and proven s
wrong with Lazarus's death.

Martha's anguish was genuine as she looked down at Jesus
and her unspoken reproach filled her soul.

Why, why did you not come in time to save him? You coul
have snatched your friend from the jaws of death and us from
the wretched grief of parting: yet you did not come. Now you ar
too late, she said to herself as she looked down at him.

She stood awaiting his reply, deeply enmeshed in her ow
frustrating pondering. Yet somehow she could feel herself bein
captivated once more by the intensity of Jesus' soul-searchin
gaze upon her. *He is so hard to resist,* she thought and found
moment of peace.

Martha looked down at him, and he seemed to be bathed in a
aura of dignity even though he was seated beneath her at he
feet. There it was again, an incredible majesty which covere
him with a royal mantle. Somehow, even with her dark well o

oughts, Martha gleaned a vague measure of hope.

It was this small seed of hope which prodded her to state, "I now that even now, whatever you ask of God, He will grant ou."

She had faith in him, but it was a faith with some reservations. ary had been right when up on the roof she had accused artha of limiting Jesus' powers. But a change was taking place thin her, and standing here, looking at what Andrew and the hers called the "long-awaited Messiah," Martha's faith increased, and her thought process began a bending toward a new rection.

Jesus smiled up at her as if he could see and measure the anging as it occurred within her, and he reached for her hand.

Martha needed no prompting. She gave him both hands and elt down on the grass beside him.

Later she was to say of that time, "In that moment I began my rrender."

Andrew and the other disciples hushed their talk completely d gave Jesus and Martha their full attention.

Still holding her hands, Jesus straightened his back and sat ect and still before her. His words were spoken in a low voice t rang with unmistakable, ultimate authority.

"Your brother will rise again."

Martha smiled and thought, *Spoken like my good father, a vout Pharisee.* Part of her religious training on the Messiah, e Kingdom of Heaven, the immortality of the soul, and the lief in life after death flashed before her mind. She was pleased sus would console her in her loss. Martha shrugged her shoulrs and warmly responded, "Oh, I know that he will rise again the resurrection on the last day."

"Martha!" Jesus cried impassionately, and his eyes ghtened her with their piercing magnitude. *"I am* the resurrecon and the life."

The words *I am* thundered at her.

Martha sat there, daring not to speak or move, for she had ever heard him speak so fiercely. His words, penetrating her ul with their directness, continued. "I am the one who raises e dead and gives them life again. Anyone who believes in me,

even though he dies like everyone else, shall live again. No o
who lives and believes in me will ever die.

"Do you believe this, Martha?" The tone of his voice vibrat
through the grove, and Martha shivered.

It was not within her power to fathom if Jesus meant physic
death, spiritual death, or both, but without pausing to exami
his deep utterance, her obedient, if not blind faith, supplied t
answer.

"Yes, Master. I believe you are the Messiah, the Son of Go
the one we have so long awaited."

They fell silent, and a peaceful pause restored the tranquilli
of the grove. A few moments later Jesus asked of Mary a
expressed a desire to see her; so Martha excused herself and l
them to fetch her sister.

She had gone only a few yards when Andrew fell into st
beside her. They walked quickly, but Martha took advantage
their private moment.

"Andrew, there is a small lump of hardness in my brea
because I still do not understand why Jesus did not come to s
us when Aaron gave him our message. Did he express his re
sons to you? What happened up there in Perea?"

Andrew scratched his head, pursed his lips together, a
finally answered, "Martha, my friend, we were just as puzzl
by it all as you. In fact, we still are.

"When Jesus heard the boys' message, he continued to tea
as if nothing had happened. We did not understand then, nor d
we two days later when he abruptly announced at our morni
meal that we would go to Judea.

"Some of the men objected to our going. They reminded Jes
that only a few days earlier the Jewish leaders in Judea had tri
to stone him to death.

"I, myself, questioned why he would risk such a foolish ve
ture and asked him directly if he really was going back the
again.

"Jesus' only answer was confusing. He said that during t
twelve hours of his daylight work, he could walk in safety, b
cause the strength and powers of his duty, which was the will
his father, would keep him from harm.

'Then he puzzled us even more, for he told us that Lazarus
d gone to sleep and now he would go and awaken him. We
sumed he meant a natural sleep, and one or two men rejoiced
t Lazarus was getting better. But Jesus shook his head sadly
d corrected us all by plainly telling us that Lazarus was dead,
t sleeping.

'But then Jesus said the strangest thing of all.''

'What was that?'' Martha had stopped, and she took An-
w's arm.

'Jesus looked at all of us and said, 'For your sake, I am glad I
sn't there, for this will give you another opportunity to be-
ve in me. Come, let's go to him.' When Thomas heard these
t words of Jesus, he threw up his hands in resignation.
omas is a good man, Martha, and a loving man, but he is ever
spondent and constantly looking on the darker side of things.
wever, we could not help but smile when he said, 'Of course,
's go too; so that we may die with him.'

'Then we broke camp and traveled here.'' Andrew ended his
zzling explanation with a shrug of his shoulders.

Martha gasped, ''Then Jesus knew all along that my brother
s dead!'' She had no further opportunity to explore the start-
g possibilities of her statement, for they had reached the nar-
w gate off the side street. Both slipped through the opening
d walked under the back portico.

'Andrew, wait here,'' Martha whispered. ''I shall slip around
d enter the house from the front doors to avoid arousing sus-
ion. Mary and I will have to leave by the front gate. I hope we
n do it quietly. We will meet you on the lower street in a few
ments.''

As she rounded the side of the house, she nearly collided with
ron and Jude astride a magnificent light-colored horse.

'Oh, Claudius is here!'' she said out loud, and the boys'
aming eyes confirmed it.

hat's good, she thought. *We need a warrior to protect Jesus.
s disciples, strong men that they are, do not seem like fighters
pable of rescuing someone who is about to be stoned to death*.
Claudius stood as tall as Peter, but he fairly bulged with well-
veloped muscles. Even when he was very young, he could

throw a spear farther than any soldier in his legion, and
wielded his dagger into action faster than an eye blinks. His d
hair was cut in the short, blunt cut of soldiers, and not only
impressive physical attributes, but his dark handsome lo
helped his fast rise in rank. Because of his well-filled body
height, he began as a young lad in a cavalry regiment, and
love of horses blossomed and developed. Quite by accident
fell into a staff position for a legate, and learned to write
creditably that he became a magistrate as well.

Martha had no trouble at all understanding how he eventu:
became the youngest tribune in the Jerusalem area. His sk
looks, and good fortune provided everything he had dreame(
as a small boy. He envisioned himself as a soldier of high ra
and he had achieved his dream.

Because Claudius and his men had been assigned to patrol :
keep the peace in the temple area, Jesus was no stranger to h
It was there, in the outer area of the temple, that Claudi
heart was first moved.

He told Martha and Mary later, "As I looked and listene(
this man called Jesus, I experienced the first pangs of jealousy
was as if, with all my rank and power, I had nothing compare(
this man. Where I had never wanted before, I now felt an ev
widening void, and I found myself staring at the walls in
quarters at night, wondering if what I possessed was worth a
thing at all."

Martha had never heard him say outright that he was a
lower or a believer of Christ, but certainly he was a friend. !
was relieved to know he was here and hoped she would find I
quickly.

As inconspicuously as possible, Martha hurried through
courtyard and into the main entrance. With no more tha
raised eyebrow, she signaled Mary to come to the doorway.
the same moment she realized Mary was talking with Claudi
so she motioned that he come too.

Martha stepped outside into the courtyard gardens and wai
impatiently for them to untangle themselves from the others
Finally, in what seemed to Martha an eternity of time, M
and Claudius sauntered over to Martha. In guarded whispers

ld them of Jesus' presence and that he had asked for her. Mary
ould have fled instantly to the grove, but Martha restrained her
d said, "There is a need for secrecy and silence, my sister.
ur friend Jesus' life is in jeopardy, and we must proceed with
ution." Then, turning to Claudius, she said urgently, "You
e a soldier, familiar with the ways of battle and evil men.
ease—for us—see to his safety."

Hastily Claudius told them he had heard the ugly death rumors
Jerusalem, and that Martha's request was unnecessary. "I am
rue, but secret, believer of Christ," he said. "Weeks ago, as I
tened to the preaching of Jesus, my inner emptiness became a
ality.

"Once I heard him say to ask, for it would be granted; to seek,
r you would find; to knock, for it would be opened; so, without
lling anyone, I asked. I asked for the Kingdom of God to fill my
ing and take up the emptiness. I do not know how this was
ne, but it was accomplished." As he talked, he walked be-
een the two women, and the three slowly strolled to the outer
tes, unaware of several Jewish leaders following.

"I have committed my soldiering skills to Jesus' welfare and
fety," he finished.

Everyone assumed they would turn to their left, go up the hill,
d spend some time at the tomb. Instead, the three turned right
d walked down the hill in the opposite direction to meet up
th Andrew. The mourners were astounded and hurried to
tch up with them.

When they reached the grove-garden, Mary broke from
artha, Andrew, and Claudius and ran almost blindly to find
sus. When she reached him she flung herself at his feet, weep-
g, and a great love spilled out of her as she expressed her inner
arnings.

"Oh, Lord, if you had been here, my brother would still be
ve!"

Martha heard Mary repeat her own statement as she reached
em and marveled that when Mary said her exact words, they
unded so different. There was no accusation in Mary's tone,
ly a weeping sadness and loving regret.

Jesus pulled Mary to her feet. She was sobbing uncontrol-

lably, and to console her, he put his arms around her. Past h
head he saw Martha, Andrew, Claudius, and a host of Jewis
leaders.

Martha took in the sight of all that love and misery, the pit
able spectacle of bereavement, the utter futility of human cons
lation at such a moment, the mourning Jews standing near th
trees who watched Jesus' every move, and she understood ful
the strong emotions which shook Jesus' frame with a powerf
shudder.

His voice was choked with sadness and almost savagely h
cried out, "Where is he buried?"

Mary was still weeping and clinging to his shoulder; so Marth
stepped over to him.

"Come and see."

He lifted his head up and the sun, filtering down through th
feathery gray green olive trees, glistened on his face and bear
as they were washed with his tears.

He then bent his head, said something to Mary, and afte
nodding at his disciples, Jesus, his friends, and the crowd o
mourners began their walk to Lazarus's tomb.

Martha and Andrew led the way with Jesus a few steps behin
followed by Mary. Claudius stayed close to the little group bu
remained in a position clear of the men to see trouble before
began. Martha was not so far ahead of the group to miss hearin
Rabbi Ben Isaiah and the others talking of Jesus.

They were agreeing among themselves that Jesus was a clos
and dear friend of Lazarus. Rabbi Ben Isaiah commented, "Se
how much he loved him. His tears prove it." Then the tenor o
the conversation changed, and Martha couldn't see who, bu
someone, in a voice close to sneering, asked: "This fello
healed a blind man. Why couldn't he keep Lazarus from dying?

Martha burned with conviction, because the man's questio
echoed her very own thoughts of a few days ago. She hope
Jesus had not heard, but he had. In that moment he stoppec
turned around, and with angry, fiery eyes bore into the man wh
spoke. No one could tolerate the thrust of Jesus' stormy emotio
or his anger at the ghastly work of death; so momentarily the
stopped, midprocession, and dropped their eyes to mutely star

t the dust about their feet. The moment passed, and they re-
umed their walk.

By the time they passed the house and had almost reached the
omb, Martha noted with some dismay that the procession
welled with almost all of Bethany's inhabitants.

Now, keeping his presence in Bethany a secret will be impos-
ible, Martha thought. *Why don't they just leave us alone?* In-
tead the procession picked up more people at each turn of the
oad, and eventually they all reached the rocky hill and stood in
ront of the family's tomb. Jesus turned to some men standing
ust behind her, and to Martha's dreadful horror, she heard him
sk the men to roll the stone aside.

Nothing he could have done would have shocked her more.
h, dear Adonai, she breathed, *we buried him the same day he*
ied because of our ovenlike climate. His soul has utterly de-
arted from his moldering, decomposing body, and I am not
eady to reveal the shocking spectacle or bear the embarrass-
nent if that tomb is opened. He must not open that tomb.

Frantically she rushed at Jesus crying, "My Lord, my Lord,
vait. By now the smell will be terrible, for he has been dead four
ays!" Past him she saw several heads bob up and down in
greement.

Jesus looked at her with patient compassion and solemnly
sked, "Martha, did I not tell you that if you believe, you will
ee the glory of God?"

She looked upon his face—the face of all truth—and unable to
esist or deny him, she spun around, and to the men she curtly
napped the order, "Do as he said. Open the tomb."

Then, attracting no one's attention but Mary's, Martha delib-
rately raised her veil over her head and wound it securely over
er nose and mouth. Mary followed suit as she had been silently
irected.

After they recruited several more to help, the men finally
noved the stone aside, leaving the entire entrance unbarred.

Jesus left Mary and Martha and walked just up to the edge of
he entrance. Everyone else backed up and shrank away, but no
ne took their eyes off the figure in front of the dark and silent
omb. A great hush fell on everyone. No human spoke or

moved, and even the earth's wispy sounds of birds, insects, a
winds were settled and stilled.

Jesus stood facing the dark cavern and lifted up his eyes to t
heavens above and immediately thanked God for hearing h
prayer.

Martha pondered later that it was almost as if he had prev
ously prayed and given his request to God, and God had alread
answered.

Then Jesus seemed to direct his prayer to Martha and all t
others who stood by, because he prayed, "And I know that Y
always hear me, but on account of the people around here, I sa
this so that they may believe that You have sent me."

Martha and Mary stood together, arms locked behind ea
other's back, their veils drawn tightly over their faces. Th
could only stare and wonder at him, their strange and remar
able friend, Jesus. They could not believe their ears when
moment later, in the briefest of utterances, Jesus cupped o
hand to his mouth and simply called, "Lazarus, come out!"

Mary buried her head in Martha's shoulder, not willing to s
or hear anything from this dreadful place, but Martha stared
the back of Jesus and geared herself for the sickening odor
decaying flesh. It never came.

Jesus took a few steps to the side, and now the dark entran
was clearly visible. At first all they could see was just a blac
hole. Then a grayish figure rose slowly off the bench inside t
entrance. Sluggishly the figure dragged itself upright and stiff
shuffled its way to the opening.

Martha's heart pounded and raced within. She shook Ma
and fiercely whispered, "Look . . . look!"

Everyone moved together, as one silent mass, closer to t
entrance, and as if they had one pair of eyes, they saw the wh
binding cloths which wrapped the tall figure of a man. The
watched in utter disbelief as the figure tossed his head veh
mently to shake off the head napkin, and instead of the repulsi
odor they expected, the air was filled with the fragrance of h
ointments.

Jesus had not watched the cave or the emerging figure but ha
turned to observe the faces and reactions of the people. When

...w they were stunned, motionless, unable to speak or move, he
-oke the silence, smiled, and, pointing at Lazarus, com-
anded, "Unbind him and let him go!"

Martha heard him first, and, leaving Mary, she sprang to aid
.e figure. She grabbed the head napkin and gasped with hazy
:cognition.

"Lazarus, is it really you?" The words clogged together in her
:roat. The color of his hair and his eyes was the same, but his
:in had lost its pallor and was of a healthy hue. His eyes were
ancing in brightness with the absence of pain.

His smile was broad, and he teased, "Martha, will you stand
:ere all day or will you help me out of this?"

Now she was laughing and crying all at once. She began un-
.inding the wide strips of cloth, and over her shoulder she called
. Mary, "It's our brother—Lazarus—come see!"

Mary and the others moved forward, not quickly at first, but
autiously. Finally the truth of it all began to come upon their
.earts and minds like a magnificent sunrise, and everyone began
.lking at once. Their voices began in low murmuring tones and
.creased until it was the sound of a roaring lion. Some began to
:ng; others wept or joyously laughed; little children clapped
.eir hands as if they had discovered a new game; still others
.npulsively began to dance, but no one was still.

Jesus stood off from the tomb, and as two little boys darted
.ast him, he caught one and set the laughing boy up on his
.houlders. Everyone's glorious tumult shook the little hills of
.ethany.

Somehow Hannah pushed her way through to Martha's side,
.nd together they stripped the grave clothes off Lazarus's body,
.aving him standing in his wrinkled white tunic which was
:ained with the precious burial ointments.

When he had both arms and legs free, he opened his mouth
.nd gave a whooping shout of joy to the sky above. Then in
.elirious ecstasy, Lazarus grabbed Martha with one arm, caught
.lary in the other, and whirled them about through the crowd of
.en, women, and children in an explosion of flying dust and
.kirts. All the while he was shouting, "I am alive; you are alive;
.e are alive! Praise be to Jehovah, the giver of all life!"

When he finally put them down, Martha managed to catch h
breath, and her questions tumbled out of her. "But how do y
feel? Is there any pain? Are you alright? How are you?"

"My sister," he said in a loud voice, "I am hungry—tha
how I am—hungry."

Martha clasped her hands together, not really daring to b
lieve what she heard; so she repeated, "Hungry? You are hu
gry?" She had waited all his ailing years to hear him say tho
words, and now he was standing before her saying, "Yes, de
sister, go make me a feast!"

Then, with the corners of his mouth curving in a mischievo
smile, he said in mocking confidentiality to Mary, "After all, o
sister Martha has not fed me in how many days?" Mary was st
awestruck; so she said nothing but held up four fingers.

"Ah, yes, Martha has not served a scrap of food to me in fo
days; so I *should* be hungry." He ended by hugging and danci
both Mary and Martha through the crowd all over again. He w
so newly awakened and so filled with pleasure at seeing Ma
and Martha, he had not glimpsed Jesus or really seen any of t
large group around him.

Jesus still carried the little boy, but from one side of the tig
circle of people which surrounded Lazarus, he called loudl
"You may feel hungry, and you look well enough, but I dare sa
you smell like a young maiden who has just been anointed wi
perfume for her wedding day!"

In the same moment all the humor and laughter of all the ag
before and still to come settled down on Lazarus. He realize
that his friend Jesus was responsible for bringing his soul a
body back from death's grave. That realization and Jesus' happ
words made Lazarus's face beam with understanding, and out
his mouth came a burst of incredible laughter. It rang like a hu
orchestra of trumpets, bells, and clanging cymbals, and its vc
ume was almost deafening.

Even as he laughed he ran, arms outstretched, the few ste
into Jesus' waiting embrace. Jesus put the small boy down, ar
the two men met, soundly clapped each other's back, ar
shouted together. Then, flinging their heads back, they we

sorbed in an exhilarating, yet holy, kind of contagious laughr and joy.

Suddenly, seeing Lazarus and Jesus carrying on together like is, Martha, Mary, and each person in the crowd began to owly fathom the ramifications of what they had just witnessed.

A dead man was now alive, well, and even laughing. The agnitude of Jesus' power was certainly evident when he made e blind man see, the lame child walk, and the lepers clean and ee of their hideous disease, but this—this with Lazarus was fferent, they reasoned to themselves.

Rabbi Ben Isaiah and a small group of men began to excitedly lk and question together as to how much power it would take raise the dead back to life.

Logically and systematically they ruled out prophet, mere acher, and good, holy man, and came tentatively to the word *essiah*.

"His power over life and death is not a trick. I know Lazarus as dead. Now he is not only alive, but never have I seen him so ell, so full of good health. This Jesus must be who he says he , the Messiah, the Son of God." Rabbi Ben Isaiah was making e incredible statement. He was saying words he certainly ever ever expected to utter. Yet in the face of today's extraorinary experience at the tomb, how could Jesus be anything but e Son of God? He reasoned all this aloud to the old men of ethany as they stood listening and stroking their beards as they ondered his words.

Martha caught his words and found herself marveling at the ld rabbi's willingness to reverse his theological position. *He as always said the claims of the carpenter would have to be roven and today,* Martha thought, *what better proof?*

She was still caught up in the whirlpool created by Lazarus's eturn and the crowd's high emotions when her own thoughts epeated themselves to her.

"What better proof?" and with a profound new insight she aid to herself, "I have admired and loved Jesus as a friend. I ave served him, sometimes too diligently, but obediently, and I ave believed in him. But after today's proof I find I have not

loved, served, and believed him completely and wholly witho
reservation. I need to see that my devotion to him and my ser
ing to him must not only be done because he is my friend, b
because he is my Lord." The truth—the whole truth of God
began to illuminate each dark little corner of her mind. *I mu
serve him not out of duty alone but cheerfully, willingly, and o
of love.* Her thoughts astounded her.

The incredibility of knowing Jesus for the better part of thr
years and missing his lordship, his divine saviourhood, his tr
identity poured over her soul. *How could I have been so blind*

"Dear Lord," she cried silently to herself as her eyes four
Jesus in the crowd. "You are not just my friend—you are m
Saviour, my Redeemer, my Lord. You are God come down
flesh to me, to my brother, sister, friends—no, even to the who
world. How could I have been so close to you, yet almost misse
you?

"You were here with me in my house and in my village, but
was always outside your love rushing wildly about.

"You were here within me, but I was not with you. You calle
me, but my ears were stopped, and I was deaf to your pleadings

"I did not sit at your feet with Mary, because I would not sto
my serving long enough to listen to you.

"But today, here at the tomb, you have broken past my dea
ness; you have bathed me in your forgiveness; you hav
wrapped me in your splendor; you have taken the blindness fro
my eyes.

"I do not know why I came to love you so late, my Lord. But
do love you, and I know who you are now, Jesus of Nazaret
You are my God, my King, my Saviour, my Messiah."

The wonder and depth of her words overwhelmed her. Marth
uttered a small cry out loud, and with new understandin
thought to herself, *Oh, Lord, that is why you sent the messag
that Lazarus's sickness would not end in death, but in givin
glory to God. Here, today, in your prayer you said you wer
doing this so that the people gathered here would believe.*

*Lord, did you know I would be one of those believers? Did yo
know what today would be for me?* Martha looked at Jesus, an
she knew he had heard all her thoughts, for he raised his hea

odded silently to her, and his smile was filled with warm compassion and total understanding.

"So you knew," she said aloud, and from somewhere deep inside her, a small burning fire was smothered out; a hard rocky place at her waist was instantly dissolved; the band of tightness round her chest was snapped forever. Martha stood free—hardly daring to believe the freedom.

She might have stood there forever except that she was jolted back to life's realities by Lazarus, who leaned close to her face and with eyes twinkling in merriment said, "As I said before, dear sister, I'm hungry! Let's go home and feed everybody."

"Yes, of course," she almost shouted. Martha grabbed Andrew's arm and said, "If I am to feed him and this group, I shall have to do it quickly. Come with me to the fish market. Perhaps they have not closed their shop, and I pray they have some fish on hand. You can help me, old fisherman, to select the freshest fish!"

Andrew said nothing, but immediately left the others and took long strides to catch up with Martha as she rushed briskly down the hill ahead of all the others.

The last remark she heard was made by Rabbi Ben Isaiah. The rabbi kept looking and pointing at Jesus, saying, "He is the One! He is the One!"

Martha turned to Andrew and said, "For once our rabbi has said a truth without using a cartload of words." They both laughed.

"Andrew," she said as they neared the bottom of the hill, and her face showed lines of concern, "there is something happening inside of me. It's a queer, strange thing, and I scarcely can explain it. But up there on the hill, at the tomb, I . . . ."

"Yes?" Andrew gently prodded.

"Well," she was hesitating ever so slightly. "It's just that I find it hard to believe that I have known Jesus for almost three years; yet today, Andrew, today I really saw him. And what's even stranger is that I feel so different, so . . ." she fumbled for the word, "ah, changed. I don't seem to be myself. I like this newness, but suddenly it is all a little bewildering. Furthermore, a song seems to be beginning inside of me."

"Well, sing it to me then!" laughed Andrew.

"Me? Oh, no, I've always left the singing to Mary. You se
this is not like me. Besides, I don't think I can sing."

"Have you ever tried?"

"Of course not!" she answered instantly. "I told you I'm n
the singer in the family."

"Oh, Martha, I don't care, and the song doesn't care, so si
it." She hesitated, so Andrew went on. "Remember the night
first came to your house to tell you about Jesus?"

She nodded her head.

"Then you should also remember how you kept telling n
how different I was and how well I spoke, putting words t
gether when all you could remember of me before was my eter
nal silence! What you had forgotten was that I had met, see
and given my life to Jesus, the Christ, the Redeemer, Saviour
the world, and, having done so, I was changed. Remember I st
looked like Andrew, the fisherman, but the very marrow of m
bones began a transformation, and the hidden but raw place
inside of me began to mysteriously heal.

"I am sure Jesus did not eradicate the old Andrew in me
Instead, he began to pull out those qualities, character traits, an
abilities that I never dreamed were within me. It has been
growing process which, to this day, has not stopped.

"I suspect you, dear Martha, have always been able to sing
but you had no song. However, because of him you not only wi
sing, but your ears, deaf until now, will hear, all around you, th
different miraculous music of God!"

She clasped his hand in hers in understanding, and they swun
their arms skyward. They looked like two happy children, an
whether it was appropriate behavior for a woman in her station
in life or not, she called out to a man who peered down at ther
from a rooftop, "Rabbi Ben Isaiah says Jesus is the One
Lazarus, my brother, back from the grave, says Jesus is th
One, and Andrew and I say it too. He is the One!"

The man, sleepy from his afternoon nap, scratched his hea
and tried to make some sense out of Martha's words. However
when he heard her singing he was genuinely surprised! He
voice, filled with a deep, husky richness, was loudly bringin

orth the haunting minor strains of a song. Not only had he never
eard Martha sing, he had never heard the song itself, nor did he
eally understand a word of it!

By the time Martha and Andrew reached the fish shop, the few
illagers who were not up at the sepulcher heard her song which
pilled out of her like a waterfall of crystal clear mountain water!
: was an extraordinary song, sung by Bethany's most unlikely
inger, but it was borne out of an extraordinary event; so she
ang:

> He is the One!
> Jesus, the anointed One.
> He is the One!
> God's beloved Son.
> Yes, he is the One!
> He is the One!
> He is Messiah come.
> Messiah come!

As they picked out two large fish for roasting and gathered all
ne dried, salted fish that was left into a large basket, the mer-
hants from the other small market stalls gathered together. All
ley could say, as they shook their heads in amazement, was,
Is this the voice of our Martha of Bethany?''

But of course that was before they heard the unbelievable
ews of Lazarus.

9

THERE were many astounded witnesses to Lazarus's prepo￾terous, death-defying walk out of the dark tomb, and indee
many, like Martha, seeing with their own eyes, believed on th
man and the miracle they saw.

But others did not.

A few days after what seemed to Martha a time of constant
cooking everything in sight for the ravenously hungry Lazarus,
small dark and forbidding cloud floated onto their horizon an
overshadowed their newly found joy.

Claudius was the first to speak openly about it with them.

Martha had always assumed his arrivals in Bethany routine
coincided with Jesus' visits, but later, when he came una
nounced and by himself, Martha suspected it was not total
Jesus or even she or Lazarus which drew or held his interes
The village gossipers had already begun to comment on th
tribune's slightly moonstruck look whenever Mary was about

But this day Claudius was grim, and his stern countenanc
matched the authority of his short red uniform, his brass helme
and the gleaming sword which hung at his side.

His large frame was looming above Mary and Lazarus in th
courtyard when Martha saw him. As she reached them, Claudiu
was saying, "Yes, on the day of your resurrection, Lazaru
many did believe, but, my friends, there were others who carrie
their angry, alarmed reports directly to the Sanhedrin i
Jerusalem." He spit out his words contemptuously.

"Those hypocritical men in that council—they meet in a spir
of hate and perplexity. They cannot deny that a miracle ha
transpired which has restored your life, Lazarus, but they wi

136

ot believe on him who performed it.

"Right now they can only surmise with considerable dread, bout the ever-growing influence of Jesus. They fearfully conjecure that Jesus will use this raising of Lazarus to proclaim himelf a king. Then, of course, every one of those old foxes realizes hat if Jesus does take his throne as king, the Roman government vill have to intervene. If that happens, their political existence ould be annihilated. Even now it's severely threatened.

"One of my Roman friends reported that the Sanhedrin vainly aged in impotent discussions until Joseph Caiaphas addressed hem. How vile that man is!" Claudius smote his fists together as f he wished Caiaphas had been a small fly smashed upon impact.

"But he is our high priest!" Lazarus put forth, implying the ;oodness and holiness of the office.

"It means nothing," Claudius retorted agitatedly. "Ever since /alerius Gratus made him high priest nine or ten years ago, eplacing Annas, you Jews have hoped the sincerity of heart, the ift of prophecy, and the holy honor would still linger upon the riesthood. But I tell you, it is not so with Caiaphas. As your Rabbi Ben Isaiah has privately said, 'The glory of the Lord has leparted from this one!'

"My friend Phileros, whose presence was not detected, saw nd heard with his own eyes and ears the diabolical plot of that ld snake, Caiaphas, when he spoke a few days ago.

"He said Caiaphas arrogantly stood before the Sanhedrin and vith a shameless avowal of his most selfish and unjust policies, aughtily told everyone that all their proposals about Jesus' fate vere words of mere ignorance. 'Fools' he called them. Then oudly he hissed that the only thing to do about this man was to acrifice the victim!"

"But," Mary searched Claudius's face for answers, "did no ne speak in defense of Jesus? Was there not one who stood up or him or told of the wonders he performs?" she asked.

"Yes, two men tried," Claudius said, "but old Elias added 'ood to Caiaphas's fire by saying he'd heard it rumored that esus was planning to use the Passover festival to declare himelf King of Israel.

"Murmurs of agreement rose from everyone there, for they

already knew that large masses of people follow Jesus even now.

"Finally, before it was settled, two men—Joseph of Arimathea and Rabbi Nicodemus—tried to change Caiaphas' mind, but it was all in vain.

"Even Joseph's argument that Jesus had publicly stated that his kingdom was not of this world went unheeded.

"Nicodemus went on record to say he had heard the Nazarene preach, and he had seen with his own eyes, sick men, women and children healed once they were touched by him. My friend Phileros said there was a shocked and appalling silence that followed when Nicodemus ended his plea by suggesting they all consider that Jesus might be who he said he was—the Messiah. Someone shouted, 'Never!' and then many cried that Jesus was a blasphemer. At that point, Phileros said, the chamber was filled with one heated argument after another. 'Blasphemy! Jesus is guilty of blasphemy!' Their words became angry screams.

"Caiaphas raised his hands to stop the cacophony and gradually they settled down in an uneasy silence to listen.

"Caiaphas dismissed all dissenting arguments. He did not even pause to investigate or define the victim's innocence or guilt, nor did those who sat before him. They simply accepted unhesitatingly, Caiaphas's voice of authority, and with only Joseph and Nicodemus as exceptions, the Sanhedrin council agreed to a secret order which decreed that Jesus must be put to death.

"However," Claudius wearily continued, "within hours Phileros told me their badly kept secret of a human sacrifice was out. Now Jesus lives with a price on his head."

Claudius walked away leaving them with their faces clouded in fearful disbelief, and he sank down heavily on a marble bench beside a flowering oleander bush.

The three of them just stared at Claudius as he held his head in his hands.

Lazarus was the first to break the morning's stillness. "I cannot believe they will actually carry out their vile and evil threat."

A low groan escaped from Claudius's chest, and he mur-

nured, "It is no idle threat, and they will carry it out, my friend.
They will."

"No, it cannot be," Lazarus asserted. "According to the law
now, we, the people of Israel, may put a lamb or a goat to death,
but not a man. Caiaphas cannot bring about Jesus' death."

"Then I must remind you," Claudius said slowly, "that while
Israelites are not allowed to carry out the death penalty in this
occupied country, we Romans know no such limitations.

"Caiaphas and the whole Sanhedrin can pronounce Jesus
guilty and condemn him to death. Then all they have to do is
present the charges to Pilate, and the Roman government will
carry out the sentence at their own discretion. They can even
decide what degree of punishment—from a light scourging with
the whip to . . . crucifixion." He finished the last word softly.

"But we know from Lazarus's glorious return, beyond a
shadow of any doubt, that Jesus holds the power of life and
death in his own hands. I say he will not allow Caiaphas, his
men, or soldiers to take him." Martha spoke the words and was
firm and practical in her thinking.

Up to this point in the conversation, Mary had stood by listening with her lovely blue eyes clouded with questions and fearful
thoughts. Then quietly but clearly, she jarred their memories.

"What we seem to be forgetting is that Jesus himself has
continually alluded to his death. Has he not stated privately to
several that he is to die, that he will not always be with us? I
wonder if he already knows Caiaphas's plan and has accepted it
as a part of his destiny for some reason."

Mary's insight was beyond sorting out; so for a moment they
were simply quiet, each of them wrapped in his own thoughts.
The turtledoves continually cooed their murmuring, for the
news did not disturb their morning rituals.

Claudius returned them to reality by saying, "I don't know if
Jesus has known before of their plans, but I am sure he knows
now as he has already departed from Jerusalem."

There was a sharp intake of air from the three of them, and
with their eyes they questioned him for more details.

Claudius was holding his helmet, and he fidgeted with the
plume of bristles on it as he spoke. "I saw Andrew before the

sun rose today. He was gathering provisions for their journey
He said to tell you in secret that their destination is the obscur
little village of Ephraim on the edge of the desert. He als
cautioned me to tell no one else of their whereabouts."

Then, directly to Martha, Claudius said, "Andrew sends yo
his salutations, and he gave me this message. He said, 'Te
Martha to keep singing.' I don't know quite what he meant b
that."

Mary stopped a small giggle midthroat, and Martha blushed a
crimson as a sunset.

"I didn't know you sang, Martha," Lazarus said grinning.

"I really don't," she muttered and turned her head so h
wouldn't see that her eyes had brightened at Andrew's message

Mary hugged her sister, and winking over Martha's shoulder
she said to Lazarus and Claudius, "She doesn't sing for jus
anybody! Only Andrew."

Their merriment was short-lived, because Claudius said, "
suspect if the disciples and the Master ever needed a song it i
now."

A disturbing silence fell about them. "I hated to see ther
leave," Claudius continued, "but my army discipline and train
ing in the art of soldiering confirms that their move is a wise one
I do not see how anyone could protect Jesus from death if h
continued his public ministry so openly among the vast throng
of people."

The doves finally silenced their cooing as the heat of sprin
began to settle down around them in the courtyard; so wit
Martha leading the way, the four of them retreated to the coo
interior of the great stone house.

For the rest of the day and even after Claudius had gone bac
to his headquarters in Jerusalem, the brother and his two sister
huddled together praying and reasoning over the strange turn o
events concerning their friend and Lord.

Martha noted with some relief that life went on for the nex
few weeks with a return to some normalcy—if indeed it coul
ever go back to the old way, what with Lazarus filled to the brim
and overflowing with all the good health he never had. A brie
smile flickered across her face as she thought about his newl

wakened life. In fact, Lazarus began putting on weight which
was partly due to his enormous appetite and partly because of
Naomi and Martha's gleeful devotion to making up for all the
years he idly picked at their cooking.

While thoughts of Jesus never left their minds, they couldn't
help but be caught up and consumed by the euphoric joy of
seeing this beloved one. Lazarus had been so frail and sickly,
but now he was not only alive but bursting with a healthy
countenance and frame!

Spring was fully upon them all. To Lazarus, it was his first
season of good health, and he took full advantage of his strength.
Together with Joseph, he tramped over the countryside inspect-
ing fields and searching for newborn lambs that might need assis-
ance. His days were long, rich, and full of captured dreams.

To Mary, ordinary days glittered with wonderment, but spring
days were shouting festivals of joy! Now with Lazarus alive and
well it also meant a time of rapturous praising to God and a time
of discovering all the flowers which were bursting with fragrant
blooms. She listened to baby birds valiantly trying out their new
voices, and several times she roamed the back hills, carrying her
sandals in her hand, so she could feel the newness of spring as
she walked barefoot in the velvetlike emerald green grass.

Spring, to Martha, was all of those things too, but only in a
small way. To her spring meant one thing and one thing alone—
cleaning!

Clearly she reveled in it and thoroughly looked forward to it.
By the time the Passover feast would arrive, her house would be
ceremoniously, religiously, and immaculately clean. It would
also "sparkle and shine enough to blind a person" as Lazarus
had often said.

It was true, but Martha felt a new exuberance about the whole
thing. Washing, cleaning, and polishing were things a person
could do and really get his teeth into. It was practical, and it
was needed; so spring cleaning was rewarding to her sense of
doing. She loved it. Together with the servant girls, Martha
worked tirelessly, and no nook or cranny was left untouched.

Over the years, Deborah, Leah, and Tabitha had collected
lovely treasures for their labors. Always after Passover, Martha

put action to her appreciation, and the gifts she bought the gir
made the long hours of their work seem like only fleeting m
ments.

This spring Martha gave herself to cleaning with a new aba
donment. It was while Tabitha was holding a small carpet, an
Martha was flailing away at it with a sturdy stick that Tabith
ventured, "You are really enjoying this cleaning, aren't yo
Mistress?"

The dust Martha was beating out of the rug was getting int
their clothes, hair, eyes, and mouths. Martha stopped, looke
over at Tabitha and then down at her own dress, and laughin
said, "I'm taking this too seriously again, I see."

The two women walked back into the house with several sma
carpets in their arms, and Martha confided, "Tabitha, it's ju
that I have this feeling."

"What feeling, Mistress?"

"Well, I think this year during Passover, Jesus and his me
will have the Paschal Supper here with us in Bethany. I believ
he will come here to celebrate. He has not said he would, and
don't know why I feel this so strongly, but I do."

"Ah," sighed Tabitha. "That is why we are working so har
and falling on our pallets at night like dead flies."

In the days that followed, Martha gave herself to cleaning, b
as the house began to shine from her efforts, she began to spen
more time checking the front entrance and outer courtyard. Sh
was so sure they would come, she didn't want to miss the fir
glimpse of Jesus or his men.

Many of her thoughts during the day were of Jesus, but
night, when all was quiet, she was haunted by other thoughts

Always she wondered about Lazarus's four days in the tom
What was it like? Was he alone and cold? Was he afraid? On an
on the questions paraded before her.

She decided it was unseemly of her to ask; yet never ha
anyone known a person to return from the grave. So she rea
soned, *Why not? It's a once-in-a-lifetime opportunity—but wh
if my questions embarrass him, and he refuses to answer?*

Finally, when she could stand it no longer, at an evening me
when the last bite of lamb stew had been finished, and the de

cate spice and honey cakes had melted away in their mouths, Martha boldly began her questions. It was what all the rest of them wanted to know but were too timid to ask.

Their friends, the widow Hannah and the neighbor Simon, were guests that evening, and since they were old friends, Martha decided to go ahead and speak her mind.

"My brother," she began, "I do not want to offend you or cause you any distress, but we have never known or spoken to anyone who has come back from the place of waiting. Our curiosity blows through us like a strong wind. Tell us what it is like to die." When no one spoke she added, "So when our time comes we may meet death with a knowledgeable dignity."

Her statement, perfectly phrased, suddenly set off an avalanche of inquiries from the others, and their questions about his dying tumbled out.

Mary asked immediately, "Did you see Mother and Father?"

"Was it dark and cold?" queried Simon.

"Were you frightened and alone?" This from the widowed heart of Hannah.

"Did you see God?"

"Wait," Lazarus cried and in good humor held his hands over his ears. When they settled into stillness, he apologized. "Forgive me, I should have known you would wonder, and I should have told you about it before this."

"Begin at the beginning," said Mary, her hands clasped under her chin, elbows perched on the table, and her eyes wide with anticipation.

"The beginning? Ah, yes. You were singing that silly but wonderful song about Jesus coming to our house. I was listening when I slowly realized I was not in any pain whatsoever. It was a new experience for me, and it was a very peaceful thing to simply lie there listening to your voice.

"Then your song faded away; so I looked over to see why you had stopped, but instead my eyes saw a most wondrous sight!

"Mother and Father were standing at the end of my pallet! Their faces were wreathed in loving smiles, and they beckoned me to get up and go with them."

"You really did see them? You were with them?" Mary's

eyes were spilling over with tears, and the others listened with enraptured ears. He nodded yes.

"You were not afraid—even though you knew they were both dead all these many years?" Martha questioned.

"Oh, no, there was not the slightest fear, only a growing feeling of anticipation which seemed to fill my soul. It was rather like the times I remembered from when we were small and would be getting ready to travel northward to the beautiful seashore of Capernaum. I felt that same excited desire to get started.

"It was a strange moment, for while I lay there on my pallet my spirit seemed to leave me, and it rose to meet them. It was as if I shed my physical body like a butterfly coming out of its cocoon. No pain, no fear—just an incredibly peaceful transition, and in front of me were the open, waiting arms of our beloved parents."

"Where did they take you?" Simon's choked voice whispered.

"To a distant mountain, and while I'm not sure *how* they took me, suddenly we were standing before gigantic iron gates which stood like sentinels before the mouth of a tunnel in the side of a large, barren mountain.

"Slowly the gates opened, and as we walked down the tunnel to an enormous underground cave, we were welcomed by many, many people. I couldn't begin to see everybody, there were so many, but the place felt warm and secure. And the people—oh, the people—they were beautiful. They were saints of God."

"Sheol is believed to have two subterranean parts: one place called Paradise or Abraham's bosom, for the righteous; and the other for the unrighteous," Simon said, to see if his religious training had been correct. Then he asked, "Did you see the other place?"

"No, but I had no doubt that where I was had to be Abraham's bosom, for the peace of God rested on each person like a warm woven cloak," Lazarus said, shaking his head.

"How did you pass the time of day?" Mary asked.

"That's just it, my sister. There was no passing of time—no

arises or sunsets, no need to eat or sleep. Our souls just talked
d fellowshiped with one another. That is why at the tomb, I
d to ask you how long I had been gone. I had no way of
owing."

"You weren't cold or lonely, then?" Hannah looked intently
Lazarus as she asked the question out of the depths of her
eving heart.

"No, not at all. It was, as I said, a warm, friendly place, and
re seemed to be no danger or evil anywhere or in anybody."

Martha leaned forward, "You sound almost as if you would
ve liked to remain there."

He flashed an affectionate smile at her before answering,
ou may be right about that, my sister, for during my stay in
eol, besides the wonderful people I was with and the joy of
ng reunited with our parents, I experienced the first moments
wholeness in my body. To be without pain or weakness after
many years—well, it is hard to describe."

He stopped as he suddenly remembered what he wanted to tell
artha. He startled her by grabbing her arm. "I meant to tell
u this sooner, Martha. I saw Benjamin."

She winced with the sharp pain that pinched her heart.

"Do you remember how badly Benjamin and our father were
n apart by the chariot and horse's hooves?"

"Oh, that I could forget that hideous sight, Lazarus. Even yet
ee them in my dreams." She held her hand to her breast to
se the pain. A surge of sour nausea filled her mouth.

"Well, my Martha," Lazarus's face was radiant, "I saw Ben-
nin and Father, and they have not one mark, wound, scar, or
emish on them. They are whole—as whole as I am now!"

Martha's hand flew to her mouth as she gasped, "They are
ole?"

"Perfectly whole."

The words "He restoreth my soul" swept over her, and she
ought, *How wonderful. God even restores broken bodies.*

Martha regained her composure and began slowly breathing
ain. She sat lost in her thoughts as she contemplated how good
vould be to see, for once and for all, the unblemished forms of

Ben and her father. *It would be like looking at Lazarus now,* thought. She turned toward him, and her vision blurred w happy tears.

Mary's chin was resting in her hands, and she did not m them as she questioned, "Then, with seeing everyone so v and having once experienced the wonder of Sheol, was it wr for us to wish you back here with us?"

Her keen discernment took him by surprise, but he eased worry with a short laugh and said, "I certainly might h thought so for a moment or two while I was vainly trying to unwound from those grave clothes, but one look at your s prised and joyous faces eased any doubts about returning.

"There is something else," he said and grew sober with inner thoughts. "I've just had time to reflect on and realize t but I now know I will never again be afraid of death and dying has lost its terror, for I have seen how it really is.

"You must not fear death either," he said, looking deeply i each face. "The righteous, the just, the believers need not f the transition time or the breaking of earthly ties. There's much more to come for the man or woman who loves God. not fear the moment."

He leaned back away from the table, and looking absently the ceiling beams, he finished by saying, "At this time I'm sure how I shall serve the Lord or in what manner I shall sp the rest of my days but . . . ." Then looking into their faces said, "Dear ones, he brought me back for a reason, and I inte not to fail him."

For a long time they sat there trying to absorb all his wor Each person was filled with the awesome hope of resurrecti Somehow their burdens of grief were lighter than they had e been, and old wounds were quietly healed.

10

LAZARUS was something of a celebrity, and the curious
crowds filled the narrow streets of Bethany to capacity. They
waited half the day to catch a fleeting glance of Lazarus.

The people talked of him as a man who had cheated death, and
some even believed that if they could see him or, better still,
touch him, they too would cheat and rob death of its victory. His
fame grew, and exaggerated stories of Lazarus's experience
abounded.

At first Martha was filled with an exhilarated sense of well-
being over all the interest. She desired that all who came to see
Lazarus would become believers, as she had. But as the days
wore on, the crowds increased, and her evangelistic zeal cooled.
When camel caravans were routed up the hill to her house,
Martha's enthusiasm waned and then ebbed completely away.
Bethany was no longer a quiet, restful village, and what had
been called a house of retreat, now became the town's center
place for congregating—like the main well in some villages.

Mary found Martha outside their front gate one morning, busily attacking the large mounds of camel dung with her broom.
Martha's face was stormy with a scowling frown.

"Martha, my sister," she called, ignoring all the travelers' and
visitors' inquisitive stares, "don't be so angry with all of this.
Remember the greatness of their wonder. Naturally they have
come hoping to see Lazarus with their own eyes."

Martha kept flinging her broom at a stubborn pile and shouted
back, "I am pleased with their reasons for being here, dear
sister. It is what they leave behind that angers me!"

Mary's bubbling laughter filled the courtyard and floated the startled eyes of strangers.

As the spring season slipped luxuriously into its f blossomed and ripened maturity, Martha, Mary, and Laza tried to ignore the crowds, and they rested well in the fact Jesus' hideaway was still a secret. It was known only to a s faithful band of followers, and they reassured themselves tha harm had befallen him.

The council of the Sanhedrin, however, knew no such pe and they were totally frustrated in their attempts to locate Je discreetly. Slowly the plotting men realized his hiding p would not be purposely or accidentally revealed to them; so t published an order. It decreed that if any man knew of Je whereabouts, that man should come forth and reveal Jesus' lo tion. The Pharisees were bold enough to publicly add, "So we may seize and arrest this Jesus." It was reported that e their bribes had not yielded up Jesus' whereabouts, and run raged that Caiaphas and the council were seething in anger

As the time of the Passover drew near, more people than his close followers wondered if Jesus would leave his se burrow to come to Jerusalem. Would he come, as count other pilgrims, to ceremoniously purify himself from defilen before the great feast of the Passover? Would he, in fact, join streams of caravans filled with Galilean Jews, knowing it we surely cause his death? Would he risk exposure and arrest Passover?

Martha, Mary, and Lazarus pondered these and other qu tions on the rooftop in the cool of Bethany's evenings. Ma insisted Jesus would spend Passover with them even if he di secretly. But each night's conversation left them pooling t own ignorance, and dawn's early sunrise found them tired without answers or solutions.

The only thing they were sure of was that Jesus would relatively safe during the day with great crowds of people rounding him. The Pharisees would not risk the multitue anger, especially when it was close to Passover time. Bu night, that was the problem.

Claudius had told Lazarus that if ever they arrested Jesu

ht, away from the throngs of followers, it would mean his
rtain death.

They wondered among themselves, and their apprehension
w with each day.

One morning, just seven days before Passover, their confusing
eculations came to an abrupt halt with a loud, banging noise
their front gates.

"He has returned! I knew he would!" Martha bounded off her
llet. She pulled over her head the first tunic her hand found
d ran for the front door.

Early rays of rosy sunlight were peeking through the trees in
e courtyard as she opened the outer gates.

Disappointed but cordial, she greeted their neighbor Simon.
'eace be to you, good neighbor. What brings you here so
rly?" Martha asked.

He brusquely hurried in, caught her arm, and whispered
rcely, "May we go inside? I have news of the Master."

Once inside, Simon's words burst out of him like a long pent-
stream of water.

"First, Martha, Jesus was seen yesterday with a pilgrim cara-
n in the barren gorge which leads up to Jerusalem from
icho."

Simon turned his head away from Martha as he talked. It was
old habit he found almost impossible to break.

Only two years ago Jesus had stretched out his hand and
uched Simon. It was a simple act, but because Simon was who
was, the act carried with it a sentence of exile. Simon's body
re all the mutilating marks of the scathing, loathsome disease
led leprosy. His fingers had been slowly eaten away, and his
nds had become nothing more than stiff, useless claws. His
et were scarred with ulcers, and they were so badly deformed
at he could not walk without the drooping feet buckling under
m. His nose, once large and regal, had collapsed and disap-
ared beneath the surface of his skin. The absence of his eye-
ows and his heavily wrinkled skin joined together to confirm
e ugliness and stigma of his disease.

Yet with one unhesitant, unconditional hand, Jesus touched
m, and Simon, once unclean, rejected, and even supersti-

tiously feared, was made instantly whole. In that mome
Simon had gingerly examined his fingers, feet, face, and foun
his amazement that everything had been restored to its orig
completeness in one touch, as if they dared not hesitate fo
second to do Jesus' bidding!

When he had been pronounced clean again, Simon had
sumed living with his family in Bethany, and since his kinsf
were Jerusalem merchants who worked on the same street
Martha's father and uncle, the bond of friendship was str
between the two families.

Still, he turned his head when he spoke, implying that he v
even yet unclean and full of leprosy.

Martha gently touched his face and turned it to her. "Y
always forget you do not have to worry over such things
more. Now speak directly to me, as I do not want to miss a
thing. You said you have news of Jesus?"

His smile was apologetic yet warm, and thus reassured
Martha's acceptance, he spoke directly to her, ignoring his ye
of lepers' customs.

"Yes, early this morning I found Jesus' caravan, and he t
me he will part from his train of pilgrims. I think some of
pilgrims will enjoy the hospitality of friends in the city, a
others will set up booths or tents in the valley of Kedron or
western slopes of the Mount of Olives. But Jesus said he v
come here—here to Bethany."

"I knew it!" Martha gasped, daring not to believe all of th
but desperately wishing it were so. "When?"

"Tomorrow night, just before sunset commences the S.
bath."

She hugged him impulsively and said, "Oh, we must tell
others, and I must make a great feast." She was about to be
cooking and cleaning the already spotless house when Sim
caught her arm.

"Is there something else?" Martha questioned, fearing fo
moment that all the news was not good.

"Only that . . ." he hesitated, for he had eaten at her hou
knew her reputation as a hostess, and was not too sure
reaction would be pleasant. "While you are to supervise

tire feast, for your abilities are well loved by the Master and
 of us . . . ."

"Yes?" she leaned forward, interrupting him.

"I asked Jesus if the dinner could be given at my house up the
 eet. I have never shown my gratitude for all he has done for
 , and I wanted . . . ."

"Oh," Martha laughed in a breathless burst of relief. "Is that
? Of course, dear Simon, we will grant your request. It will be
 your house, and I shall see to the food; so the feast will be the
 est in all of Bethany!"

Then with more insight than he knew he possessed, he tilted
 head to one side, and looking at her thoughtfully, he said,
Martha, you are skilled in cooking, serving, and seeing to
 ers' needs, but somewhere along the way you have acquired
 gracious grace of genuine hospitality, and I salute you, my
 ighbor."

She was unaccustomed to compliments concerning her be-
vior, especially as to having "gracious grace," but seeing that
 was serious, she meekly replied, "I thank you for noticing."

As quickly as possible, Martha escorted Simon out the door
 d through the courtyard to the gates, so she could rush back to
 l everyone the news.

The day passed in a rush of furious activity, involving trips to
 market and continuous trips from her cooking area to
mon's house and back again. Mary was recruited to get con-
ners full of water; so they'd be ready for flower arrangements
 following day. Lazarus and Joseph were dispatched to take
 the wooden stools up the hill to Simon's house, for an over-
w of guests was expected, and everyone was pressed into a
 rry of flying feet and busy hands. Their exhilaration ap-
oached the point of silly childish giddiness, but such was their
 , and they abandoned themselves to the enormous task of the
nquet.

By late afternoon, the day of the banquet, Martha had
 ipped everything into perfect order.

The cucumbers, leeks, and onions were all washed and
 upulously free from blemish or dirt. Both plump ducks,
 ked clean inside and out, and a large selection of quail were

securely fastened to the roasting spit, and already their jui⟨
were dripping and hissing onto the bright coals below, makin⟨
delicious aroma.

Joseph brought in two wineskins from their underground c⟨
lar cave, and Martha pointed both him and the skins in ⟨
direction of Simon's house.

Mary cut and artistically blended the long flowering branch⟨
of tree blossoms into her readied pottery jars and bronze va⟨
to make Simon's house a house of color and fragrance.

After the richly brown crusted fowls were taken up ⟨
Simon's, the final touch was added by Martha. She took ⟨
assortment of small bowls to add to Simon's table, and wh⟨
that was accomplished, the banquet was ready.

Martha had worked as hard as she ever did in planning a⟨
executing such a feast, but Jesus' words about her serving ar⟨
somehow, her experience at the tomb had taught her some s⟨
cial lessons. Remembering the dire consequences of fatigue, s⟨
saved time to rest and refresh herself.

There was even a sweet time with Mary, involving wheth⟨
Martha should wear the blue dress with the darker blue bib a⟨
girdle or the flaxen-colored one with its brightly embroider⟨
green accessories. They laughingly chose the flaxen one ⟨
Martha, because the green girdle reminded Mary of the brig⟨
yellow green of spring and of Lazarus's fresh new life! The tv⟨
sisters laughed together as if they were little girls playing th⟨
game of hide and seek once more.

Finally, when they were all dressed, the two sisters a⟨
brother made their hurried way up the hill four houses ⟨
Simon's, but it was not the usual quick easy walk.

Somehow, between word of Jesus' suspected arrival and t⟨
unbridled curiosity concerning Lazarus, many people throng⟨
the streets. Passage through them was almost impossible. Th⟨
someone recognized Lazarus, Martha, and Mary, and the thr⟨
thought they'd be trampled to death.

By some high-stepping maneuvering, they managed to get ⟨
Simon's house and were relieved when the gates opened ma⟨
cally, and Simon's arm reached out and pulled them quickly in⟨
his garden.

The house had no separate place for dining, but it was spacious, and the table was set up in the large common room. Martha's quick glance before she and Mary reached the cooking area confirmed that all was ready, and her face glowed with satisfaction.

They were both arranging some dried fruits on large trays when a servant boy breathlessly told Martha that Jesus and his men had arrived.

The women hastily took off the towels around their waists and went to greet the guests. Martha was impressed and humbled by the assembly of men before her.

Jesus and all of the twelve disciples were there as well as a few faithful believers. Among others, there were distinguished men like the Rabbi Nicodemus and Joseph of Arimathea. Martha nodded her shalom to Andrew above the heads of Matthew and James, but in all the hubbub she knew she would have to wait to actually speak to him.

Simon and some of his servants were all given to the washing of feet and hands, and greetings were warmly being exchanged when Mary and Martha slipped up behind Jesus and touched his arm to make their presence known.

Martha would remember later that night, after everyone was settled on their pallets or in their sleeping quilts, how startled Mary's face had been when Jesus turned around to greet them. Mary's lovely skin had turned ashen in color, but there was no time to ask what she saw in Jesus that troubled her; so Martha simply greeted Jesus and then, excusing herself to the cooking area, left them together.

There was no decision to be made as to who the governor of this feast would be, for Simon himself put the specially made robe upon Jesus and led him to the bench of honor. However, surprising Lazarus completely, Simon motioned that Lazarus would sit right beside Jesus as the next honored guest. It was a splendid beginning, and Simon's broad, beaming grin grew even wider as the first of many courses began to be served.

Martha was absorbed in her delegating duties and pleased beyond reason that everything was going exactly as it should. This was a new feeling for her. She was actually loving every

moment of all the scurrying about, the comings and goings of
servants, and her ears were gently stinging with the lavish pra
the guests were pronouncing about the food.

For some time she did not notice Mary's absence, and th
when she did, she caught sight of Mary slipping through the ba
entrance carrying one of the family's all-too-familiar boxes
perfumes and burial ointments.

"Why have you gone home for that?"

But her question to Mary was lost because Naomi shove
large tray of roasted duck into Martha's hands and said, "Th
need this." Martha took the tray into the large room and v
immediately immersed in many duties, and her questioning
Mary was pushed quickly out of her mind.

It was toward the end of the meal, after the big woven bas
trays of fruit had been served, that Martha came to a dead h
and stood motionless as a statue to watch her sister.

Mary had never looked so strikingly beautiful. She was we
ing a long, full-sleeved tunic which was the fragile shade
apricots, and the girdle at her tiny waist was a lavish tribute
her embroidering skills.

The pale, delicate coloring of her dress contrasted harmo
ously with her flaming golden-red hair, and she was enchant
to see, but all who were present were quite unaware of l
exquisite face and form. In fact, most of them did not see l
clothes, her hair, or even her delicate, fair skin, which v
stretched over her high cheekbones in flawless beauty. Th
only saw the tears. Mary, for some reason, was unable to c
tain her weeping and her lovely blue eyes were spilling out l
sorrow. The tears were streaming down her face now in a t
rent.

As Martha and the others watched, Mary softly but purpos
walked over to where Jesus was eating and stood behind hi
Carefully she broke the seal on the alabaster box she held a
then removed one of the glass vials. After she set the box on t
floor, she broke the vial and poured its redolent contents
Indian spikenard into her hands. Without spilling or wastin
drop of the precious ointment, Mary let it slowly spill first ov

us' head, and then, kneeling down beside him, she massaged
ently onto his feet.

No guest spoke or moved. Even Peter, who usually gave a
nning commentary to most everything that happened, was un-
plainably mute. Nor did Jesus himself protest verbally or
ke any physical move to stop her.

Martha searched Jesus' face and thought she saw what
med to be a look of resigned sadness as if he alone under-
od the full meaning of Mary's actions.

t was clear from their faces that none of them understood
y Mary had used her burial ointment. Martha's heart con-
cted a little at the sight of the box. Of all the treasured things
 father had provided for his children, the three alabaster
xes filled with rare and costly perfumes, to be used at the time
their deaths, were among the most precious.

Lazarus's box is empty, and now so is Mary's, thought
rtha, but, like the other guests, she remained silent and
tchful, unable to comprehend the significance.

As she watched, Mary deftly undid her hair. With one or two
ck movements she slipped out the pins and small comb that
d her hair which was coiled at the nape of her neck. In one
athtaking second the silken red tresses spilled out and over
 shoulders, catching all the dancing lights of the lamps and
dles in the room. They all saw this, and there were heard
ps of appreciation.

Mary seemed oblivious to everyone's presence save Jesus',
 in one exquisite moment of self-abandonment she bent her
d and with her long flowing hair dried his feet.

Mingling her tears with the precious spikenard, Mary was
aware of the others, her family, or the genuine treasure of
grance which was now filling the entire house.

Years later they would say of the night that the feast was
morable not because of the large number of Jews who
onged to witness it, nor primarily because of Jesus' visit, or
 newly returned-to-life Lazarus, but because of a woman's
phetic act of loving sorrow which signaled and marked the
ginning of the dark and dreadful end for Jesus.

Martha saw the whole drama played out before her with r
eyes of love. Mary, with her dazzling beauty, her bell-like si
ing voice, and her creative hands, was always the center
attention. For years Martha was known only as "Mary's siste
and sometimes, when she stopped to think about it, she fe
few shivers of resentment as they crept about in her mind.
everything inside her had changed that day at the tomb. It wa
if her love for the Lord had been a smoldering, smoky ash h
that, instead of dying out, had suddenly erupted into a blaz
flame. She was free to love—especially Mary—as she had ne
been able to before. If they called her "Mary's sister"
would be alright. In fact, it would be most pleasing, and
sensed a newly found pride.

Martha found herself acquiring a surprising taste for patier
and for the first time she began to understand her desire to b
comfort to the sick and dying instead of merely applying a p
tice or brewing an herbal remedy. But most of all she had
covered some brand-new characteristics in herself: like sing
the song which bubbled within her, or feeling a new devel
ment which involved a risk—that was the decision to give her
in love to others. She became more tolerant of people, and to
surprise, she began to accept them as they were without imp
ing on them her frantic desire to change them.

So it was, as Martha watched with eyes of love her sist
simple act of humble adoration, her heart beat with love
pride in an unexpected tempo.

Martha was so engrossed in the beauty of the scene that
was in no way prepared for the reactions of others present in
room that night.

She overlooked the fact that most of the Galileans who
lowed Jesus were unaccustomed to any luxury. They were te
bly aware and genuinely concerned about the use of the co
contents of the alabaster box. Their amazement that the
cious gift would be intemperately lavished and wasted on
brief moment knew no bounds. After the stunned silence
ebbed away, they could not contain their anxious grievances
longer, and a murmur began to rise from all corners of the roo

Seated right behind Martha was the loudest voice of all.

ad his back turned to her, talking with the others, when in a
udden burst of agitation he spun around and stood up just an
m's length away from her.

He was one of the carefully chosen men named Judas Iscariot,
nd his pink cheeks, framed by a cherubic round face, gave no
dication of the depths of his inner ugliness. Older Jewish
omen patted or pinched those cheeks in chucking admiration,
ut the dark rumors about his being a petty thief never ceased.

"This is not a gesture of love, but an odious, repulsive act of
aste!"

Martha's mouth dropped open, aghast at Judas's blatant pro-
ouncement. She could not begin to understand the vehemence
his voice as he continued.

"That perfume was worth a fortune."

Martha, very well versed in money matters, having discreetly
arried on her father's vineyards, olive groves, and sheep herds,
uickly assessed the value of the spikenard at three hundred
enarii. By Martha's standard of wealth it was certainly *not* a
ortune, but just as she thought that, someone she could not see
aid reproachfully, "It must have cost three hundred denarii.
nd we know one denarius is a whole day's wage for a laborer."

Judas was shaking his finger at Mary's bowed figure bending
ver Jesus' feet.

"Think of that. Three hundred denarii! It should have been
old, and the money given to the poor and to the destitute!"

Martha's cheeks were burning although she did not know
hy. She was glad Mary had done what she did, but there
eemed to be some truth in Judas's scathing words.

Andrew rescued her and her thoughts by gently pulling her
own to sit on a low stool he had found.

"Oh, Andrew, I know not what to think," she whispered.

He leaned over, and in a sarcastic tone of voice she had never
eard before, he said quietly, "This is the first time I've ever
eard of Judas's concern for the poor. I wouldn't pay too much
ind to him. I have a feeling he speaks out of guilt from some
alicious or perhaps wasteful deed of his own."

It was a shocking thing for Andrew to say about one of the
ethren in the closely knit group, and Martha would have ques-

tioned his accusing manner, but Jesus spoke.

He held his hand on the top of Mary's still bowed head an looking directly at Judas, said, "Let her alone." His voice wa inexpressibly sad.

Martha sat looking at him and thought it was as if he would n permit Judas's worldly indignation to spread any further amor the listening disciples. Nor did he seem willing to let Mar already the object of unfavorable looks, suffer any more co sequences from her noble act. Martha was always amazed at h ways. Whether there was a mob of people or one person, Jesu spoke with complete understanding.

"Why do you trouble the woman, Judas?" His look pierce Judas's soul, and the angel-faced man, deflated by truth itsel sank down upon his bench. But Jesus was not through; so, mo ing Mary gently aside he stood up and addressing them all, I said, "Mary has done a good and beautiful thing to me. As to t poor . . ." he pointed his finger to the people assembled the and said patiently, "you will always have the poor with you, a whenever you wish, you can do good to them. But you will n always have me."

Then, looking down at the small, crumpled figure of Mary t his feet, he nodded toward her, and his voice filled with a te derness which would later haunt their memories as he compa sionately said, "She has done what she could. In pouring th ointment on my body, she has done it to prepare me for buria Truly, I say to you, wherever in the whole world this Gospel preached, what she has done here tonight will be told in memo of her."

The friends and followers of Jesus sat still, hardly knowin what should be said or done next. Martha felt Jesus' words ha delivered yet another deathblow to her expectant messian hopes. Almost as if with one mind, the guests began to unde stand no earthly wealth would be realized, and Martha clear knew certainly no kingdom or regal elevation could be attain by following one who was so soon to die.

Peter agitatedly pulled at his beard while shaking his head n James, Philip, and John huddled together, whispering. Othe sat still, trying to fathom it all.

Since she could think of nothing to say, Martha, puzzled as
e others, began clearing away the large trays. Most everyone
quietly murmuring among themselves as she stepped in and
und them, but she continued to gather the trays in an effort to
ep busy, thereby avoiding the thoughts of sadness which were
ce more pushing in around her. She could never understand
w quickly things changed around Jesus. One moment it was
preme joy to see him; the next moment would bring sorrowful
estions.

Martha was just about to walk through the doorway to the
oking area when she collided with Judas. The tray with left-
er fruit on it spilled all over before she could catch it.

"Out of my path, woman," he snarled as he struggled to keep
s balance. Finally catching himself against the wall, he righted
mself and gingerly stepped through the mess of fruit and trays
out his feet as he ran for the back entrance.

Both Peter and Matthew saw the incident, and Martha looked
them questioning, "What does that offensive man have to do
th you disciples? You are not like him."

Matthew bent to help her as she picked up stray fruit and
attered trays.

"I do not know, Martha, but our Lord chose him, and he is
e of us," Matthew said stoically. Then kindly he said, "Which
e of us, Martha, least of all me, a tax collector, knows the
pths of Jesus' love or why he chose any of us?"

It was a gentle rebuke, and she accepted it meekly.

Peter walked to the doorway, peered out after Judas, and then
me back. He was as thoughtful and as quiet as Martha had
er seen him, and she listened carefully when he spoke. "I
n't know about him," Peter said.

"Judas's suggestion has not only been thwarted; he has been
blicly silenced and implicitly rebuked. He looked as if he had
en seized by a monstrous madness. Judas is a man who har-
rs grudges. I wonder what desperate or evil deed he will
dertake to avenge his humiliation tonight." Wordlessly
artha picked up the last of the trays and retreated to the cook-
g area until all was cleaned and put back into order. She would
ave it to the men to sort it all out.

The next morning she greeted the dawn with sleepy eyes a heavy limbs. It seemed that Saturday morning's sunrise ca earlier than expected to Martha. It had been way past the n night hour before she bedded everyone down for the nig Simon's house was too small for everyone to stay; so many the disciples spent the night at her house. As she peered ou her latticed window, she saw many people gathered in the str and muttered, "Well, what new and surprising thing will this e bring?" Then, brightening a little, she said out loud, "As Da said, 'This is the day the Lord has made, and I will rejoice and glad in it!' " Her thoughts added, *Even if I don't like all the people milling about out there.*

Evidently Jesus' presence in Bethany had become gene knowledge overnight, and consequently everyone guessed t after the Sabbath, he would most certainly enter the Holy C Martha could sense the feverish excitement which was alrea running through the crowds even though Saturday's sun v barely over the first hills. The day was spent quietly in spite the growing excitement, and Jesus conversed with them as e ily as he taught them.

At the dawn of Sunday's sunrise, Jesus, all his disciples, an few neighbors gathered at Martha's house for a light morn meal.

Mary hurried out back to the cooking fires and said to Mar and Naomi, "After we break bread Jesus is going into the c this morning. He said he will teach in the temple today."

Naomi continued to place the hot barley cakes in a large basket, but Martha stopped abruptly. "Does he not understa the seriousness of Caiaphas's and the Sanhedrin's charge? will be arrested, and who knows what hideous fate awaits him

"I think he knows but the knowledge seems only to make l more determined," Mary said quietly. Then she shocked Mar to her very core when she said, "I want us to go with him t morning. We are his family here, and we should stay togethe case there is trouble."

"But the crowds of people . . ." Martha sputtered, "I do fear arrest, but I do fear the thought of being trampled to deatl

"Martha, we of all people, because of Lazarus, have the m

son to be loyal to the Master. We must go with him, not to
otect him, we would be of little help, but to put feet to our
ve."

Her argument could not be denied; so it was decided that after
e meal, they would accompany Jesus into Jerusalem.

Their meal together was short, but there seemed to emerge a
aceful fellowship between them. A sweet holy peace en-
loped each of them. It was short-lived.

The crowd outside the gates gave a great shout of recognition
en they glimpsed Jesus coming through the flowering trees of
e courtyard. They were ready and prepared to receive and
lcome this Deliverer who had raised Lazarus from the dead.
t Martha had seen the fickle ways of a mob before down in the
zaar of Jerusalem, and she knew their minds were capable of
ise one moment and stoning someone to death in the next.

They started out on foot with Jesus out in front, flanked on
her side by Peter and Andrew, but almost instantly the crowd
allowed them up, and Martha lost sight of Jesus. Once,
omentarily, she glimpsed Andrew's deep red hair over the
ads, but the surge of people was so great that nothing re-
ined in one place for very long.

Almost immediately Lazarus was separated from them. So
artha determined she and Mary would stay together, and
htly she gripped her sister's arm.

Martha knew all about the three roads that led from Bethany
er the Mount of Olives to Jerusalem. One pass was between
e northern and central summits; another way ascended the
ghest point of the mountain and sloped down the other side;
e third road, which was always referred to as the main road,
ept around the southern shoulder of the mountain's center
d lay between it and the Hill of Evil Counsel. Since the first
o routes were more mountain paths than roads, and Jesus was
rrounded by disciples, friends, and crowds, Martha was re-
ved when he took the third route. *It is easiest by far and
lay,* thought Martha, *we will need all the ease we can get.*

The crowd of people grew in size almost immediately. It was a
le frightening because people were shoving and jostling each
her for a better glimpse of Jesus.

Martha heard a whole group of them chanting Lazarus's na[off to her right and wondered where he was and how he w[faring in all the commotion.

With the palm and cypress trees of Bethany behind them, th[went south and approached some large fig gardens. The fig tre[were the only thing Martha could see, but she knew instantly t[small village of Bethphage was near.

By some maneuvering between excited men clamoring fo[look at Jesus, curious women and children, and bewildered d[ciples, Martha finally pressed in a few paces behind Jesus. [was talking to Peter and John. She searched the crowd [Lazarus and Andrew but did not find them. Then she hea[Jesus say something about going into Bethphage and bring[back a colt. Peter was saying, "But Lord . . ." and then abo[the shouting she heard Jesus clearly say,

"If anyone asks what you are doing, you simply answer, 'T[Lord needs it and will send it back soon.' "

Peter and John nodded and pushed their way out of the tigh[compacted circle around Jesus and went off to the village.

Everyone milled around, some asked questions of Jesus, [they could get close enough. Others strained for one look a[then excitedly described Jesus to their friends standing by.

To Martha's mind it was an impossible circus, and she que[tioned why she had ever agreed to come.

Mary's face was glowing, and Martha could not imagine wh["Mary, how can you be so calm? This crowd is madness itse[One minute they are practically kissing Jesus' hand, and the ne[they are nearly trampling him and us to death."

"But these people," said Mary, gesturing to the crowd arou[them, "are believers! They know he is the Messiah. Surely y[would not deny their happiness at being here, would you?"

"Believers?" Martha snapped. "No, I think they are on[pilgrims here for the holy week, bored today, and seeking a[entertainment they might find."

Mary had no chance to answer because Peter and John we[back with a young white colt.

When he reached Jesus, Peter took off his outer garmen[threw it over the colt, and helped Jesus up onto its back. "[

eans to ride into Jerusalem on the back of a young, probably broken colt?'' Martha gasped.

As if it were a signal of trumpet blasts, the crowd seemed to ow a triumphal procession had begun.

No sooner was Jesus mounted when the many people around n took off their outer garments as Peter had and spread them a tapestry path before him. They began lifting up their voices praise, and their spirits were absolutely jubilant.

Mary looked at Martha for one long moment and mouthed the ords silently, ''See, they are believers.''

Whatever they were or whatever they had was contagious, cause Martha, shaking her head and smiling, joined in the aising.

Many people tore or cut down olive, fig, and walnut boughs om the trees which grew in abundance in Bethphage and scat- red them before him. Even the disciples put away their long ces, and without stopping to fathom the whys of the crowd's bilation, they too joined in.

Martha, Mary, and all those about them burst into exuberant outing:

> Hosanna to the Son of David!
> Blessed is the King of Israel
> that cometh in the name of the Lord!
> Hosanna in the highest.

Everyone caught up the joyous strain. Many in the crowd gan telling marvelous tales of Jesus' acts, and others told how sus had raised Lazarus. ''Yes, even that one,'' they said as ey pointed. Martha managed to glimpse Lazarus with James d John. He waved a quick hello, and then suddenly everyone as moving.

The road before them sloped by gradual ascent up the Mount Olives through green fields and under shady trees, until it ddenly swept northward. It was there at that angle of the road, e magnificent city of Jerusalem burst into everyone's view.

Martha was a little breathless from the climb, but the sight of e city always robbed her of any breath she had left. Both

sisters stood on the crest of the hill trying to capture its love
ness forever in their minds.

There, before them on that sparkling clear day, rising out
the deep shaded valleys which surrounded it, the city of t
thousand memories stood outlined before them. The morni
sunlight as it blazed on the marble pinnacles and golden roofs
the temple building blurred their visions with fiery splendor.

Such a glimpse of such a city was at all times deeply touchin
and no Jew could pass that spot without voicing his praise. B
that day with Jesus their emotions were too heartfelt for spee
as they stopped to gaze. Even the ever-growing, noisy crow
quieted. It was then in the clear morning's stillness that a lo
cry cut the air. The first cry was followed by wailing, sobbi
sounds.

"It is Jesus who cries!" said Mary, her face ashen white.

Up until now, Jesus had sat majestically but completely sile
in the midst of all the adulation. He neither smiled, nor frowne
nor commented, but his large grey blue eyes were wide with t
reality of scriptural fulfillment.

Martha heard Jesus and said to herself, *Always there is my
tery about him. One moment we are rejoicing that this is t
Messiah, but the next moment we are not too sure. Does
Messiah or king weep over his kingdom?* She wondered.

Martha did not understand why, but while Jesus had we
silent tears at the grave of Lazarus, now he wept aloud. It sent
cold chill down her back in spite of the hot, sunny day.

He not only wept, but his voice choked and broke into
passionate lamentation. It was a strange messianic triumph and
confusing interruption in the midst of festive hosannas.

Someone behind Lazarus shouted, "The Deliverer wee
over a city which it is now too late to save, and the Ki
prophesies the utter ruin of a nation which he came to rule!"

Jesus, still weeping, exclaimed, "Would that you had know
personally even at least in this, your day, the things that mak
for peace!" Then sorrow interrupted his words, and when I
found voice to continue, he could only add, "But now they a
hidden from your eyes. And it is too late." Every person wa
now listening intently to Jesus.

He stretched forth his arms in the direction of the great golden temple and said, "For the time is coming to you when your enemies will throw up ramparts around you and will encircle you and besiege you and your children within you to the ground and will not leave you one stone on another, because . . . ," here he paused for a moment, shaking his head in great sorrow. "Because you did not understand when you were divinely visited."

Jesus finished his lamentation, and without question, they knew the pause in their procession was over. Puzzled and filled with rising doubts, they continued their walk.

Martha and Mary moved away from the center core of the large group and made their way to one edge of the crowd as they descended down into the valley.

They could see a multitude of people below them. There were people from all over Israel camped down in the valley of Kedron and about the walls of Jerusalem. Almost at once the pilgrims whose booths and tents stood so thickly on the green, grassy slopes below caught sight of the approaching company, and they knew immediately who it was that traveled towards them. A cry of recognition spread among them.

The people tore down the green and graceful branches from the great forest of palm trees which surrounded Jerusalem, and they streamed up the road to meet the Prophet. Soon the two companies of people met—those who had come with him from Bethany and those who had come from Jerusalem. Amid many waving branches and shouted hosannas, they accompanied Jesus into Jerusalem.

Martha and Mary were caught between both groups and once more a great wave of joyous shouting went up, and again Martha felt it was a circus run wild.

"See, they love him too." Mary was confident no harm would come to him with such loyalty and affection.

"But the mood of a crowd is ever changing." Martha's thoughts grew dark.

Both Andrew and Lazarus caught their arms, and for the rest of the walk, they accompanied Martha and Mary.

When they reached the walls, the whole city of Jerusalem was stirred with powerful excitement and alarm.

"What is this?" the citizens asked, peering out of their la
ticed windows, looking down from roofs, and standing aside
let them pass through the narrow bazaar streets.

To her dismay, Martha heard someone answer hesitantly, "
think it is Jesus, the Prophet of Nazareth."

She wanted to shout up to them in their windows and ign
rance, "It *is* Jesus of Nazareth alright, but he is the Messiah, o
long-awaited King."

However, the words stuck in her throat. *What's the matte
with me,* she wondered. *I know he is who he says he is. So why
this foreboding fear gripping my soul and paralyzing my speech*

*Is this shadow of uncertainty and fear falling on everyor
else?* She questioned herself and searched Mary's face to fir
answers, but Mary was busy. She was excitedly talking wi
Claudius.

He had ridden up with other soldiers, spotted her, di
mounted, and now was listening to her as she described the
walk from Bethany.

Later Martha, Andrew, and several others would mark th
day as a day of Zechariah's prophecy fulfilled, for he said in t
Sacred Writings, "Rejoice greatly, O daughter of Zion! Shout
daughter of Jerusalem! Behold, your King shall come to yo
righteous and victorious, humble and riding on a donkey, on
colt, the foal of a donkey."

But at the time within the city gates and walls on that brig
sunny day, it was safer and wiser to say Jesus was merely
prophet from Nazareth.

Martha and several of those who followed closely were begin
ning to feel the first real pangs of doubt, and a dull kind
disenchantment began to set in.

Martha's heart was sore afraid.

11

WHEN the excitable populace streamed before Jesus through
Jerusalem's city gates, Martha and Mary decided to return to
Bethany. They pushed through the crowd to Jesus, so they could
take their leave and bid him their farewells.

The Master was still surrounded by a multitude of people and
many of his disciples, but it seemed to Martha that he sat on the
ass's colt all alone as if no one were near. He was, as he had
been throughout the journey, quiet and pensive. With the excep-
tion of his lamentations back on the crest of the road, he spoke
to no one. As she came face to face with Jesus, Martha saw that
the marks of the tears he had wept remained on his cheeks and
his beard glistened with wetness. His skin was grayed, even in
the bright sunshine, and Martha's nature, instinctively quick
with herbs and medical remedies, rose within her. Desperately
she wanted to get him inside a shelter and give him some herbal
tea, but because of the crowd, she only blurted out, "Master, it
is not safe for you to stay here in the city. When you have
finished in the temple, will you spend the night in Bethany?"

He nodded silently at her and then, not attracting anyone's
attention but hers, he placed one finger across his lips so she
would know it was to be kept a secret.

With that the women pushed through some men, spotted the
head of Andrew above the others, with Lazarus close by, nodded, and called their shaloms to both of them before setting off
for home.

When they reached Bethany, the women entered their courtyard and sank down wearily on a marble bench to rest a few

moments. They were covered with dust on the outside and fi
with an uneasy sadness inside.

"Are you not going to prepare a supper for them when t
come tonight?" Mary asked, surprised that Martha had sat
long without a move toward the cooking area.

"No," Martha answered. "I think Jesus and the disciples
not stay here tonight with us but in the grove-garden. Too m
people know of his love for us, and, who knows, someone,
to help with Caiaphas's arrest order, might be watching our g
right now. I will send Aaron down to the grove before sundo
tonight to see if Jesus and the others are there. If they have
eaten, then I'll take care of it. At least by tomorrow mornir
shall take food down there, but for now I'm weary, and you m
be too. Let's wash and eat something."

"Yes," Mary said, her voice strained and overtired. She ga
Martha a helping hand up, and, together, they entered the hou
relieved that the long exacting day was ending. Later Aa
reported no sight of Jesus; so Martha retired to her pallet wi
out knowing that late that night Jesus and the men stole quie
into the grove-garden.

Martha rose early Monday morning before the sun star
over the first hill. By the time she filled a large basket with wh
cakes, figs, and raisins, Mary joined her, and they both w
down to the grove-garden. They could see it was too la
Everyone was gone, and only the matted-down grass gave e
dence of their overnight bivouac.

Martha chuckled softly and said to Mary, "They cheated
out of serving them this time, but I shall make up for it tonig
In fact, I think I'll set Aaron and Jude in there," she said as s
pointed to a bush thick with foliage, "to watch for them."

The next few days for Martha were quiet, and aside from t
preparations for the Paschal Supper she was making, nothi
was unusual. Jesus, Lazarus, and all the disciples continued
return every night to Bethany, and whether it was privately
her house or secretively down at the grove, the guests we
served well.

Martha was delighted to be doing what came so easily to h
but she was so busy preparing the daily food for thirteen gue

us her family and servants, that she hardly had time to listen to
daily happenings.

Eagerly Lazarus tried to tell her about Jesus as she rushed
out from the table to the ovens, but she only got bits and
pieces. Lazarus related that Jesus healed blind and lame people
the temple and told many parables and stories of real life. He
said Jesus also called the scribes and Pharisees some terrible
names, including hypocrites and snakes, but, most surprising,
some members of the Sanhedrin actually believed in him.
Lazarus had said this last part in a breathless kind of wonder.

Martha heard Lazarus just as she was leaving the cooking
area, and over her shoulder she called to him, "See, Jesus really
who he said he is!" Then she disappeared through the outer
door with a large basin of wastewater in her hands.

Only once, very early one morning, in their hurried talks
Martha noticed Lazarus had grown still, and surprisingly he was
not busily giving his report. Martha stopped stirring Naomi's
corn porridge and knelt down beside Lazarus, who was sitting
a stool. Looking up at him she wordlessly asked what troubled him.

"I'm sorry, Martha. I did not intend to withdraw or be such
poor company. It is just that I am very perplexed by some of
yesterday's happenings. It was something Jesus said." Lazarus
talked slowly and in such low tones that Martha had to concentrate to hear his words.

"We were sitting around him on the slopes of the Mount of
Olives when Jesus, in a voice calm with certainty, told us he
would be sacrificed on the very day the lamb would be slain for
the Paschal feast."

"Oh, well," said Martha easily, "you know all of us love
poetic speech, and Jesus is a master at parables, stories, and
even riddles; so perhaps he did not mean actually *sacrificed* but
meant the offering of himself in dedicated service as the high
priest of the temple."

"No. He meant slain and sacrificed." Both Lazarus and
Martha looked up to see who made the statement with such
authority, and Mary stood before them in the doorway.

"She is right," Lazarus said, over Martha's rising protest.

"But surely you don't think that this coming Thursday, t[
night of our Passover feast, Jesus will be . . . ." Martha gasp[
and clamped a hand over her mouth.

She dared not tell them that she had harbored the lovely sec[
hope that Jesus and his men would eat the Paschal Supper w[
them. *We are his family,* she had said to herself. *The feast is[
family festival. He has no family living in the vicinity [
Jerusalem; so we will be his temporary mother, father, brothe[
and sisters. Besides, he cannot sacrifice himself. It would r[
the memorial feast of the birth of our nation—not to mention r[
dinner,* she thought bleakly.

"Jesus is going to die," Mary interrupted Martha's though[
"I do not, for one moment, understand why, or how, or even [
what manner. But ever since the dinner at Simon's house, I ha[
known. When I looked at Jesus that night I could not see h[
clearly, for he was wrapped entirely in grave clothes, and [
burial napkin covered his head and face."

"So that is why you left the banquet to fetch your alabas[
box of ointments."

"Yes, my sister," Mary answered.

Martha stood up, and taking off her apron, she said sternly[
Mary, "Please serve the porridge and bread to everyone w[
has not eaten this morning, Mary. I must clear my head." S[
grabbed a dark blue veil from off a wall peg, and deftly throwi[
it over her head and shoulders, she hurried out the back e[
trance.

Martha walked with her head down to discourage anyone fr[
speaking to her, and she moved quickly over the cobblesto[
streets of the village. She was so completely absorbed in h[
own thoughts that she didn't see anyone. In fact, it was on[
when she reached the outskirts of Bethany and was paddi[
silently down the dirt path, that she realized exactly where s[
was.

Her feet had taken her through a small, tree-lined pass in t[
hills, and stretching out in front of her were the beautiful l[
hills and valleys she had loved all her life, as her father h[
before her.

She was enmeshed in the sight of sheep and lambs nibbling [

fresh green hillsides when suddenly she saw, nestled down in
e valley, three men sitting under the trees. She recognized
us immediately.

'Aha! So this is where he goes when he vanishes from our
dst.'' Martha was delighted to have found out his secret.
ten she had wondered where he went or what he did when he
t her house. Sometimes he went with just two or three of his
n, but once or twice it was alone. Seeing this valley in the
lliance of its glorious springtime, she could readily understand
choice.

From where she stood, she identified the two men with Jesus
being Peter and John. They were talking in earnest with the
ister, and as yet, they were unaware of her presence.

Martha looked away from the three men to the weeping-
llow trees behind them. Their boughs bent low and formed a
fy screen of privacy. Off to the east a few paces, water bab-
ed and tumbled in the newly filled brook.

Oh, Master, she thought to herself, *seeing you here in these
ls tells me you must hate the noisy, dirty cities where the
use and garbage is flung into the streets and where men and
avenger pariah dogs jostle each other continuously in over-
owded bazaars and thoroughfares. No wonder you love
thany so much. Here is a place where you can talk with the
ther in heaven.* Martha silently blessed God's name. Then her
oughts continued eloquently. *Here too, dear Master, under
e curtains of the willow trees, far from the disturbing sights
d sounds of the city, you can sit on the pillows of grass, smell
e fragrance of the field lilies, listen to the playful bleating of
e lambs, and watch the splendor of a sunrise or a sunset.*

The whole peaceful scene reinforced a decision she had made
deliberately. Martha strode down the hill toward them. She
cided that she would risk their displeasure at her knowing
eir sequestered hiding place and interrupt them. Whether she
ould or should not speak her mind was an issue she flung into
e spring winds.

With her head held high and in great spirits, spurred on by the
auty of the scenery, Martha marched down the valley to
here they sat.

Noisily she greeted them. "Shalom, Master and friends." S[
took advantage of the fact that they responded warmly to [
and plopped herself down next to Jesus. Everyone, even Pe[
fell silent as if she had interrupted a secret meeting, and no o[
spoke.

Martha was all prepared to launch into the issues at hand, [
as usual, the moment she looked directly at Jesus, every wo[
was removed from her mouth. Her abruptness melted, and th[
the stillness of the others caught up with her. For several lo[
moments she just sat quietly. Finally, after swallowing hard[
very subdued Martha asked quietly, "Master, may I speak w[
you a moment about the Passover?"

Nodding yes, Jesus answered, "Of course, Martha. You m[
always speak your mind with me." And finding her voice aga[
she began, "Everyone in all of Israel is thinking about the fea[
It will be a glorious Passover festival. I feel it in my bon[
Master, it is as if spring and the renewal of life all around us[
serving as an omen of good tiding." Then, glancing at two lam[
a few paces away dancing around their mother, she continue[
"I have all but the lamb prepared for the Paschal Supper. T[
herbs, haroseth paste, unleavened bread, and wine are all read[
and with my whole heart I hope it is your desire to celebra[
Passover with us here in Bethany." She searched his face a[
hoped he would be direct with his answer.

He was. But it was so blunt it stopped her breathing fo[
moment.

"We shall take the Paschal Supper in Jerusalem," he sa[
simply.

"But . . . ." She fought for logical persuasive words. "Ma[
ter, it is not necessary to travel to the city. Bethany has be[
decided by rabbinical authorities to be well within the limits [
Jerusalem.

"Besides, Lazarus, my sister Mary, myself, and your dis[
ples are like family to you." Her voice was almost pleading no[
"The Paschal Supper is a family time, and I had so dreamed y[
would be with us. It seems so feasible . . ." she ended lame[

"No, I have other plans," he said evenly.

Martha was utterly shattered. She looked at Peter and Joh[

they offered no help. Peter merely shrugged his shoulders in I-don't-know-why-either gesture.

esus saw her devastation and leaned over and touched her ulder. "Martha, Martha, I will try and make you under-nd." His voice was steady and filled with warm compassion.

"When I was a young boy, my parents, kinsfolk, and I made long trip from Nazareth to Jerusalem. It was my first trip where that I can remember, and my first Paschal feast in the / of David.

"The moment I saw Jerusalem I loathed it, for it was a horrid ht. We approached the gates, and the first thing I saw, lined on either side of the road, were the scaffolds for those who uld be executed. My heart was sickened by the cruelty of it Finally we made our way past them and up to the temple. I I been devoutly and thoroughly instructed as to the temple's ire layout, but to see it in its full grandeur filled my being with

"It is my Father's house, Martha. And even then, as a boy, I w it. The temple, made with white marble and gilded with d, was bigger and grander and filled with more people than thing I had seen in my whole life.

"It is no wonder that several days later within the confines of t splendid edifice, amid several thousand worshiping pil-ns, I was separated from my parents.

"My mother thought I was with my father, and my father ught I was with my mother. Others took it for granted that I s with our kinsfolk or mingling with the other children.

"In any case, they left Jerusalem without me, and it was not il they halted at the first night's stop in Shechem that they covered and confirmed my absence."

le smiled over at Martha, but she was too absorbed in trying nake sense of what Jesus' story had to do with his refusal to with them to notice.

"Anyway," Jesus ignored her puzzled look and continued, "I l not meant to disobey them or wander off without telling m, but I was strangely drawn to a large group of learned ctors and scribes in the temple. Normally they met in private sed sessions, but because of the Passover, their arguments

and discussions were held publicly and open for all people in
temple colonnade. They readily accepted me, and I was v
much at home with all of them.

"I was able to answer all their inquiries and theological qu
tions. I even enjoyed entering into their debates with them, a
it was as easy as if for all my twelve years I had done so.

"Eventually my parents retraced their steps and found m
Jesus now smiled broadly at the memory.

"My mother," he said, shaking his head, "was very ve
with me and told me so! Of course she had good reason, fo
was young and the dangers of a city filled with Roman soldi
and overcrowded with people were very great.

"But, Martha, my answer to my mother then, that day at
temple, is the same answer I give to you now about the Pasc
Supper—'Do you not know that I must be about my Fathe
business?' The supper will be eaten, not in Bethany, but
Jerusalem, for I must do the will of Him that sent me. I m
finish His work."

Martha contemplated his words, and slowly her mind, but
her heart, accepted his story and his reason. She wanted to
his face, but could not for the tears which blurred her ey
Finally, when she spoke, she said, "Master, it seems I've
much to learn. I am grateful for your patience. I shall be av
able to help in any of the preparations or serving should
need me. I am your servant." Rising, and ignoring the lump
her throat and the terrible ache it was making, she nodded
silent shaloms to them all and climbed the hill to the roadw
Only once she turned around to memorize the scene and th
walked quickly home.

It was late that same night, after she had retired to her pal
that Martha thought she heard something and got up to inve
gate some noises at the front gate. Lazarus heard it too, and
the time she lit a small torch, both of them saw Peter's a
John's faces outlined in the darkness.

They hushed their voices, but their words made Marth
heart quicken in wonder.

"We knew today how hurt you were about the feast . .
John started to explain, but Peter took over.

"Jesus sent us to Jerusalem this afternoon with strange but wonderful instructions. We were to watch for a man carrying a pitcher of water." Seeing a look of skepticism on Martha's face, he said, "I know that is highly irregular, Martha—a man carrying a jar of water—but just listen. We were to follow him home and say to the owner of the house, 'Our teacher says for you to show us the guest room where he can eat the Passover meal with his disciples.' "

John interrupted with, "When we saw the man with the pitcher, we walked behind him and had no idea where he was going, but we were surprised and pleased to find he is a servant of Joseph of Arimathea! We were warmly welcomed by Joseph, and his large upper guest chamber stands ready for our feast."

"Joseph sends his greetings," Peter said. "He asked us to remind you of his friendship with your father, Martha. Respectfully he requests that you come and supervise the roasting of the lamb and tend to other details of the food.

"The feast will be a private one for Jesus and us. Even Joseph and his sons have not been included, but Joseph wants every detail to go smoothly. Can you come?" Peter bent close to read her face.

"Oh, blessed be the name of the Lord," she breathed. To be of some use to the Master relieved some of the confusing ache within her throat. "Yes, of course I can come—Mary, too." Then she stopped and questioned, "The lamb—has it been purchased and sacrificed?"

"Yes," Peter answered quietly. "Judas was assigned to buy the lamb yesterday, and today, after we made arrangements with Joseph, we found Judas and took the lamb to the temple.

"After it was offered as sacrifice we laid it on staves, and John and I carried it on our shoulders to Joseph's house. It is flayed, cleansed, and ready for you to roast."

Martha was so excited she could hardly sleep the rest of that night; so in her wakefulness she kept track of all the times the owl outside her latticed window hooted his greeting. Somewhere after the count reached one hundred and thirty she slept.

Mary awakened her while it was still dark, and Martha, surprised to see Mary up and about already, came instantly alert.

They dressed, ate some wheat cakes, and together wi
Naomi, Martha placed the specially prepared bowls of harose
paste in a large carrying basket. She could see Jesus dipping t
bitter herbs into the haroseth, and she felt a deep culinary pric
Because she used only the finest nuts, raisins, and apples in
Martha's haroseth had a fame all its own. Proudly she carried
on the short walk to Jerusalem and Joseph's house.

Both women worked tirelessly all day with Joseph's serva
women, and not until all the unleavened bread was baked a
the lamb sizzled and roasted on a pomegranate spit did they res

Between Peter, John, Joseph's servants, and Martha an
Mary, there was nothing more to add and everything stood
completion, awaiting the guests.

In the soft hues of sundown they came, by twos and three
slipping in the side garden gate. Without attracting any und
attention or calling any greeting they soberly filed up the outsi
staircase to the upper guest chamber of Joseph's fine house.

Martha and Mary, with two other servant girls, stood partial
hidden behind a latticed window. They watched the processi
to count men and identify faces.

When Jesus and each disciple was accounted for and presen
the servant boys were sent up with the wine for the first cup

"Master Joseph and I want nothing to spoil this feast
Martha had admonished the servants.

"Mind you, now," Martha said, at the foot of the staircas
"Pour the wine into the cup and then stand outside the doorwa
until the Master has said the thanksgiving benediction and bles
ing over it. Then when the foot washing and cleansing
finished, come down immediately, for that will be our signal
begin to serve the Paschal Supper." They solemnly nodded
understanding.

Martha could see and hear it all in her head: the guests lyi
on plump cushions around two sides and one end of the lon
low table; the table itself covered with a fine linen clot
Joseph's most elegant silver wine chalice in front of Jesus. Sh
imagined his voice as he pronounced, "Blessed art Tho
Jehovah our God, who hast created the fruit of the vine!"

She would have liked to have savored her thoughts longer, b

hurried back to the cooking area to supervise the lifting of
lamb from the spit to the platter. She was arranging the
ted meat on a large bronze platter when the servant boys
e in, their eyes all wide with excitement.

How does it go up there?" Martha said as she wiped her
ds free of lamb's fat.

t is fine, Mistress," one boy said. The other said, a little
:hievously, "They had a small problem about who would sit
re, but they worked it out."

ne made no comment to the boys, but thought, *Oh, dear, we
'always so caught up in disputes over precedence and proce-
-. I had hoped this meal would have harmony and no
'licts.*

Mistress Martha?"

Yes?" She looked down into the boy's face.

He is like us," he said eagerly.

Who?" Martha asked.

The Master, Jesus."

small cough surfaced in her throat, but she quelled it, swal-
ed, and said, "Why do you say that?"

Because up there, just now, the Master pulled off his robe,
pped a large towel around his stomach, filled the copper
n with water, and dressed like us—servants or slaves—he
hed and dried everyone's feet!"

How like him," murmured Mary.

My son," Martha said, patting his head, "you are very per-
:ive and you are right. He is very much like you. It's amazing
slowly we older people come to know the truth of that!"

he would have said more, but Master Joseph's round face
its full white beard appeared around the wall corner. He
his sons had taken their supper in a small lower room off the
n courtyard. Now, without words his eyes asked her if it
e time to serve the Master his meal.

Martha allowed no more delays. The dinner was carried up.
boys held the savory lamb on its platter. Others took the
nd flat loaves of unleavened bread in a basket, and someone
ied the bitter herbs in a wide pottery bowl. Martha brought
he haroseth paste in several bowls, and Mary came up the

steps last with a tall pottery wine jar. Everyone wordlessly
his burden on the end of the table and withdrew.

Later, as they cleaned up the cooking area and burned
roasting spit in the last of the hot coals, Martha said to Mary
think Jesus' prediction of his life's being sacrificed will not c
true this night or with this Passover. It goes well up there.''
gestured toward the stairway.

Mary agreed. Then, for no particular reason, she turne
look at the staircase and was startled by a figure hurtling hin
down as fast as his feet could find the steps. He was mutte
under his breath, and all Mary and Martha heard was, ''
told him?'' and the words ''not a traitor.''

Both women caught their breath in surprise when the
lurched past them, opened the courtyard gate, and disappea
leaving the gate banging noisily in the darkness.

''That was Judas, wasn't it?'' Mary asked, uncertainly.

''Yes, I'm sure it was. I wonder what was wrong, and
would anyone leave the feast before it was over?'' Martha a
curiously.

''Perhaps he has been stricken with an illness.''

''No, I think not,'' Martha replied, matter-of-factly. ''
hard to know about the heart of Judas, but from the way he c
down the stairs, I suspect he is up to no good thing.''

For the better part of an hour the women worked silent
their tasks and were caught up in their own thoughts. Fin
Martha took a thoughtful look up the stairs and said, as
washed and dried her hands, ''I think I should go just to the
stair and listen for a while, lest something has gone amiss. T
have been up there so long.''

''I'll go with you,'' Mary added, taking off the apron w
girdled her.

The two women left the others and quietly stole up the st

By sitting on the very top step and stretching her neck, Ma
could see just past the doorway into the guest chamber. In
dim light she could see Jesus and John, who reclined facing
and what must have been the back of Peter's head and
shoulder.

What is happening?'' Mary tugged on Martha's dress from
step below.

They are pretty well through eating. I think the third cup of
e is about to be drunk, but Jesus is talking.''

What does he say?'' Mary whispered.

artha shushed her.

hen she did look back down at Mary to answer, Martha's
was wrinkled with frowns.

I heard what he said, but I do not think I know what he
ns. He broke apart one of the loaves of bread, and handing a
ll piece to everyone, he said, 'Take this and eat it. It is my
y which is given for you. Do this in remembrance of me.' ''

Did they eat it then?'' Mary asked.

Yes, and then he filled the cup up with wine, and before he
ed it to each one, he said something about the cup of wine
g a new agreement between God and them. He called it his
d. When they drank it, he said they were to do this, too, in
embrance of him. Then his exact words were, 'For every
you eat this bread and drink this cup you are retelling the
sage of the Lord's death, that he has died for you. Do this
l he comes again.' ''

'Died for you'?'' Mary questioned.

'm sure of it,'' Martha whispered back.

Then it will be. No matter how we try to prevent it, it will
' Mary sighed and rested her head against the wall.

or some time the two women sat at the top of the stairs—
tha, listening and shaking her head in puzzlement every
e in a while; and Mary, head still back, lost in her own
ghts.

Now he is saying his time has come.'' Martha's voice broke
stillness of the night.

ary edged closer and asked, ''What else?''

He called the disciples 'dear, dear children' and then said his
with them is brief before he leaves.'' Martha paused and
quoted him, saying, '' 'And so I am giving a new com-
dment to you now. I want you to love one another just as
h as I have loved you. Your strong love for each other will

prove to the world that you are my disciples.' "

"But where is he going? Perhaps we can follow, too," M
said, clutching Martha's arm, with hope.

"Peter just asked that," Martha said. "Jesus told him tha
could not come now, but later. I don't think Peter unders
why he couldn't follow now, nor do I, but Peter said loudl
am even ready to die for you.' " Martha shook her hea
puzzlement.

"What was Jesus' comment?" asked Mary, her head
against the wall.

"Jesus leaned across the table toward him and said ster
but kindly, 'Die for me? No, Peter. Three times before the
crows you will deny that you even know me.' "

"No, not Peter! He would not be that cowardly," Mary
firmly as she looked up at Martha.

"Mary," Martha said gently, "from what Jesus says no
think he really is leaving. Listen."

She pulled Mary up beside her, and crowded together,
heard Jesus say, "Let not your hearts be troubled. You belie
in God; now believe in me. There are many rooms there w
my Father lives, and I am going to prepare them for your c
ing. When I have gone and have prepared a place for you, I
come again and take you to myself so that where I am, you
will be. If this weren't so, I would tell you plainly. You k
where I am going and how to get there."

A voice spoke out, "No, we don't." Martha thought it
Philip's voice, but Mary corrected her. "It's Thomas," she s
and they listened as he said, "We haven't any idea where
are going; so how can we know the way?"

Jesus told him, "I am the way, yes, and the truth and the
No one comes to the Father except through me. Had you re
nized me, you would have known my Father as well. From
on you do know Him; yes, you have seen Him!" There w
pause, and then someone spoke. Mary said, "That's P
now."

"Lord, show us the Father, and we will be satisfied," he s

Jesus replied, "How long have I been with you without y
knowing me? Don't you even yet know who I am, Philip, e

r all this time? Anyone who has seen me has seen the Father!
why are you asking to see Him? Don't you believe that I am
he Father and the Father is in me? The words I say are not
own but are from my Father who lives in me. And He does
work through me. Just believe me—that I am in the Father
I the Father is in me. Or else believe it because of the mighty
rks you have seen me do.

In solemn truth I tell you, anyone believing in me shall do the
ne works I have done, and even greater ones, because I am
ng to be with the Father. You can ask Him for *anything,* using
name, and I will do it, for this will bring praise to the Father
ause of what I, the Son, will do for you. Yes, ask *anything,*
ng my name, and I will do it!

If you love me, keep my commandments and obey me. I will
the Father, and He will give you another Helper to stay with
a forever. He is the Holy Spirit, the Spirit who leads into all
th. The world at large cannot receive Him, for it isn't looking
Him and doesn't recognize Him. But you do, for He lives
h you now and some day shall be in you.

No, I will not abandon you or leave you as orphans in the
rm. I will come to you. In just a little while I will be gone from
world, but I will still be present with you. For I will live
in, and you will too. When I come back to life again, you will
>w that I am in my Father, and you in me, and I in you. The
: who obeys me is the one who loves me, and because he
es me, my Father will love him. And I will too, and I will
eal myself to him.''

Then someone, they could not tell who, said to Jesus, ''Lord,
y are you going to reveal yourself only to us disciples and not
he world at large?''

esus replied, ''Because I will only reveal myself to those who
e me and obey me. The Father will love them too, and we will
ne to them and live with them. Anyone who doesn't obey me
esn't love me. And remember, I am not making up this answer
your question! It is the answer given by the Father who sent
. I am telling you these things now while I am still with you.
t when the Father sends the Comforter instead of me—and by
Comforter I mean the Holy Spirit—He will teach you much,

as well as remind you of everything I myself have told you.

"I am leaving you with a gift—peace of mind and heart. /
the peace I give isn't fragile like the peace the world gives.
don't let your hearts be troubled or afraid. Remember wh
told you: I am going away, but I will come back to you agai
Mary heard him clearly and said, "See, Martha, he will cc
back!" Then they listened as Jesus continued. "If you re
love me, you will be very happy for me, for now I can go to
Father, who is greater than I am. I have told you these thi
before they happen, so that when they do, you will believ
me.

"I don't have much more time to talk to you, for the
prince of this world approaches. He has no power over me, b
will freely do what the Father requires of me so that the w
will know that I love the Father. Come, let's be going."

When Martha and Mary heard Jesus' last words, both wor
got stiffly to their feet. They climbed down the stairs and he
the men above them raising their voices in the magnificent s
of blessing from the second portion of the Hallel. The m
singing was beautiful, but their hearts were filled with sad q
tions and uncomfortable doubtings.

"Mistress Martha and Mary, do stay the night." Jos
stepped out from behind some trees in the courtyard and
them at the bottom of the stairs. "You have fixed and serve
fine Paschal feast, and it would honor me very much if
would accept my hospitality this night." His voice was fi
with kindness.

The women smiled but shook their heads no.

"We are grateful for the offer, Master Joseph, but it is t
that we head toward Bethany."

"But to go alone is not . . ." he began, as Lazarus ca
into the courtyard and waved his greeting. "Oh, I see you wil
well guarded," he said smiling.

Before Jesus and his men descended, Martha, Mary,
Lazarus bid their farewells to Joseph and his servants
walked home.

When Lazarus asked how it had gone, both Martha and M
answered politely but without much enthusiasm or ready un

nding. They knew what they heard Jesus say, but they could
t find the words to explain it all, so both women mutely
lked away.

'But Jesus is alive and well, even now?" questioned Lazarus.

'Yes, but clearly he told everyone in the room that he would
," Martha said wearily.

'Well," said Lazarus cheerfully, "he is the long-awaited
ssiah, and since no harm came to him tonight during the
pper, then his prediction about his death and sacrifice must
ve meant something else. Let us put away our sad faces and
wncast eyes to rejoice in this festive time." He walked be-
en Mary and Martha and pulled both women close to his
es as they climbed the hill road. "Have you forgotten so soon
s very road and the hosannas of the multitudes last Sunday?"

'No, we have not forgotten, brother. But you were not at
seph's tonight. Jesus said many strange things. He even gave
men a new commandment and a new practice for Passover. It
all so bewildering . . . ." Martha's voice trailed off as they
mbed the road under the full Paschal moon. Spring's chilly
ht air penetrated their cloaks and tunics; so for the rest of the
y they walked quickly and with resignation to the house on
hill.

he entire household slept fitfully and late the next morning,
it was good for them. Their minds and bodies were utterly
nt and exhausted.

shall never repair, thought Martha, as the late-morning sun
ured through the latticework and formed a pattern of
sscrossed gold on her pallet and floor.

hey spent the whole day of Friday quietly. Lazarus read
ne scrolls of Scripture for part of the day, and Mary finished
embroidery work on a wall tapestry she was making for
nnah. Martha prepared a large barley and lamb stew and
de two useless trips down to the grove-garden to see if Jesus
d the others had returned.

t was early the next morning, on the Sabbath, as they were
ting ready to attend the synagogue that they heard the loud
ttering of a horse's hooves. The galloping tumult brought
eryone out to the front door.

Claudius got off his steaming stallion, handed the reins
Aaron, and roughly drew everyone inside the house. Before th
could ask what he was doing, he closed the doors with a sava
kind of fierceness and stood before them, a raging tower
anger.

"What is it?" Lazarus asked, clasping Claudius's should
and shaking him.

"They have killed him! That's what! They have killed hi
Yesterday, after five trials which were a mockery to all just
everywhere in the world, they killed him!"

"Not . . ." Mary dared not finish with a name.

"Yes, the very one who brought the Kingdom of God to me
my emptiness. The one who was more alive than anyone I ha
ever known. The one who was the answer to life's pain. He
dead, gone, and he, Jesus of Nazareth, will be with us no more

Claudius sank to his knees, bent his head till it touched
floor, and in utter anguish cried, "My Lord, Jesus, I thought y
were God. Why did you let us crucify you?"

Martha, Mary, and Lazarus exchanged horrified glances, b
it was Martha who found her voice first. She almost scream
"Crucified? He was brazenly crucified like an irreclaima
criminal? You cannot mean this! Surely it was someone el
Someone who looked like him, but not him. Not Jesus . . .
Her screaming dissolved to a whisper, and she stumbled over
a couch.

Lazarus reached down, put his arms around Claudius a
helped him to his feet.

Directly to Martha, Claudius said with resignation, "No m
take, Martha. It was Jesus. I saw him myself."

The time to go to the synagogue came and went, but nobody
the great main hall moved. Stunned into the blackest kind
silence, they sat down together, each wrapped in the vicio
senselessness of it all.

Then Mary spoke, her voice erupting with sobs, as she
called for them, "The last we heard of him at Joseph's house
was singing with the others. I shall put out of my mind fore
how he died, and only remember the song and the sound of
singing."

azarus got up and slowly paced the length of the long room.
en, with both hands behind his back, and in a voice rich with
eving beauty, he quoted aloud Isaiah's words. "He is de-
sed and rejected of men; a man of sorrows, and acquainted
h grief: and we hid as it were our faces from him; he was
pised, and we esteemed him not.

Surely he has borne our sicknesses, and carried our sorrows;
we regarded him as a stricken one, smitten of God and
icted.

But he was wounded for our transgressions, he was bruised
our iniquities: the chastisement of our peace was upon him;
with his stripes we are healed."

Martha's lips moved silently with her brother's, and the famil-
memorized words of long ago made believable sense.

He was oppressed, and he was afflicted, yet he opened not
mouth; as a lamb that is led to the slaughter and as a sheep
ore the shearers is dumb, so he opened not his mouth.

He was taken from prison and from judgment: and who shall
lare his generation? For he was cut off out of the land of the
ng: for the sins of my people was he stricken.

And he made his grave with the wicked, and with the rich in
death; but he had done no wrong, neither had he spoken an
word."

At the mention of the significant word *grave* Martha asked
uptly, "Where was he buried?" She was calmer now, and her
nking was a little more practical and organized than it had
n.

"In the tomb Joseph of Arimathea had hewn for himself,"
udius answered dully.

"Was the body properly prepared for burial?" It was a ques-
n only Martha would have asked.

"No, I think not—at least, not as thoroughly as you would
e done it," said Claudius as he rubbed his forehead. "Jesus
d in the afternoon. I was called out of the city, for we had
ne trouble with rabble-rousers on the Bethlehem road; so I
s gone. Mercifully, death came quickly I was told. Joseph
d that by the time he obtained legal permission to take the
ly, it was just a little before sunset. I know Joseph purchased

a fine piece of linen cloth and that he spread its folds lavis
with a hundred pounds of myrrh and aloes which Nicoder
bought, but the preparations were hurried at best. Joseph s
the sun was setting and Sabbath was about to begin. So all
and Nicodemus could do was wash the corpse, lay it amid
spices, wrap the head in a white napkin and lay the body quic
but reverently in the tomb. Joseph said nothing could be de
until tomorrow after the Sabbath is passed.''

Martha glanced at him in appreciation for even these b
details and then slipped to Mary's side. Both women embra
each other and unashamedly wept in solemn silence.

Martha, as was her way, and because she was older, broke
weeping silence by wiping her sister's face with her skirt. Th
she said, with quiet reserve, ''Tomorrow, early before the s
rises, you will go with me, and we shall go to his tomb. We
use the ointment from the last of father's boxes—my alabas
box—and assist Joseph in any way we can.''

Martha did not extract a promise from Mary nor did she re
expect an answer, but she was pleased when Mary instan
responded, ''Oh, yes, my sister. We shall both go.''

On into the afternoon and late into the night, Claudius rec
structed the unbelievable and hideous chain of events for the
and their hearts were torn and shredded by the telling.

No one slept too well, and after a few hours of restless turn
and tossing, Martha got up and dressed long before the day
Twice she went to Mary's pallet to wake her but decided agai
it each time. Finally Mary awoke on her own, and the t
women, carrying Martha's alabaster box and other ointme
went off into the darkness down the road to the city.

It was during the darkest time of night, just before the f
streaks of daylight, that Martha and Mary hurried to Josep
house, through some back streets of Jerusalem. Occasionall
dog darted out in front of them, or they heard a baby's waili
but for the better part of their travel in the city, it was unusu
quiet.

They had almost reached Joseph's neighborhood when a s
den commotion in an alley to the left of them exploded into a
and a scream.

the darkness and confusion of the moment both women,
ly startled and frightened, clutching their precious oint-
ts, started to run. In the same instant something that felt like
ll of bedding was thrown against Martha's leg which tripped
and she went sprawling full-length down the street. She
:d over a step, and finally came to rest in a doorway. When
tha caught her breath and handed over her tightly squeezed
of ointments to Mary, she assured her, in the darkness, that
was uninjured. Martha then tried to get up, but the bundle of
ling was twisted up in her tunic.

There's something caught in my garments," she said to
y as she tried to unloosen it.

'ithout warning, the door behind her opened, and in the
ming light of a freshly lit torch a man glared down at Martha
Mary. He muttered his curses at them and told them to
e along.

mbarrassed, Martha said meekly, "Something came out of
alley and tripped me."

ien Martha reached down, lifted her skirt to untangle it, and
y cried, "Oh, God of our fathers, Martha! It is a child!"

Not much of one," sneered the man as he peered over
tha's shoulder. "It's best you throw it back in the alley from
re it came."

artha, still sitting on the ground, peeled away the filthy rags
:h were alive with lice until she got down to the dirtiest, most
ul human being she had ever seen.

He must be about two years old, maybe three, but he is so
ll and thin I cannot tell," she said, examining him. The
ciated boy was barely conscious.

He smells older than that," the man said, as he held his nose.

What is the matter with his eye?" asked Mary, wincing and
ly looking.

artha turned his head upward to see him, and her mouth
I with sour vomit.

His eye has been recently cut or burned. I cannot tell which.
aps both, but it is his limbs which are the worse."

icking out beneath a short, dirty, and blood-crusted tunic
were two little badly twisted legs.

Martha pulled off her veil from her shoulders and caref
wrapped the boy in its softness.

"You aren't going to bother with him, are you?" the old
questioned. "He's nothing but a cripple. He's been abando
like hundreds of others just like him."

"Martha?" Mary touched her shoulder. "Martha, what
you going to do? We are on an errand of mercy. Have
forgotten?"

Martha shook her head slowly, and in that moment she
gained all her composure. She knew exactly what must be de
She bent over, picked up the child in her arms, and then st
straight and tall before Mary and the man.

"Mary, I want you to go on and take care of the matter w
brought us here. I will carry this child home, for he needs a l
attention if he is to survive. You will go on without me."

"Without you?" Mary's face was aghast with wonder
cannot do this thing without you. I have never prepared a be
or even helped in these matters before. I cannot."

The man stood holding his torch and listening to the str
conversation, his head bobbing from one woman to the oth

"I know you have never prepared one for burial before,
you can do it. Have you not noticed that ever since we loo
upon Jesus and believed, our lives, our abilities, our talent
have extended their borders somehow? We are changed.
drew, Lazarus, you, me, others—we are able to do things
never dreamed possible.

"I want you to go to Joseph's house, ask for directions to
tomb, and then anoint Jesus' flesh with the oils and ointm
you carry."

"But his wounds will be more than I can bear," Mary
tested.

"You will survive it. The hand of the Lord is upon us. N
Mary, one of us must go to the tomb, and the other must
care of this half-dead child. Which will you do?"

Mary put her head down and answered softly, "I shall g
the tomb to help the dead, so you can go home to help
living."

Martha smiled. "I know it is asking much of you, my si

t Jesus' presence in our lives has made us all capable of doing
ny impossible things. We have not only changed but grown
cause of him. Anointing his body is the least we can do to
ow our love. There will be others there, I'm sure—maybe
en his mother Mary from Nazareth, or Mary Magdalene—but
vant you to go. Do this for him in his hour of need as you did
him in preparation at Simon's house not long ago."

They kissed each other's cheeks, and Mary hurried off down
e street. The man scratched his beard with his free hand, and
nuinely perplexed, said to Martha, "Woman, what have I seen
re tonight?"

'Ah, old man," Martha smiled broadly at him, "you've seen
e!"

'Love?" He was grinning in a puzzled way.

'Yes, love. You just saw love hurry down the street to fulfill
untried task. And here, in my arms, you see love about to be
rn. Look well, old man, for love says this child is no longer
andoned! Love says this boy has been found!"

He stood there long after she left him, still scratching his beard
d staring after her in the deserted street. "Why should she
re about that piece of filth?" he muttered to himself as he
sed the door of his house.

Martha was passing the grove-garden as the first pale rays of
a came up, and just before she reached home, the small bundle
e held against her breast gave a weak cry.

'It is alright, little one. Don't fear. I'll take good care of you,
d between the Lord and me, we will coax life back into these
bs of yours, and your cheeks will glow like the pink of the
se of Sharon." She hushed him with her soothing words.

How did Jesus say it exactly? she asked herself, a few steps
m her gate. *Ah, yes.* "*And so I am giving a new command-
nt to you now. I want you to love one another just as much as
ave loved you.*"

Somehow remembering his words and holding the small boy
me together in her soul as a great healing balm, and slowly
re burned a flicker of joy in her heart.

'I shall call you Lazarus," she said to the sleeping boy, "for
ugh you are almost dead, you will live and be well again."

12

NEVER, in any portion of her mind's eye, could Martha ha[ve] ever pictured the turn of events that fateful Sunday morning [...] the years that would follow.

The sun was cresting Bethany's hills when Martha push[ed] through the side gate, startling Naomi so badly that she dropp[ed] a small load of firewood she was carrying.

The sickening sight of such an abused face and such a ti[ny] bundle, so precariously clinging to life, drove all thoughts [of] mundane household chores to an immediate halt. Naomi hurri[ed] into the house practically tripping on Martha's sandals.

"Deborah," Martha called as she laid the child on a low ta[ble] in the cooking area, "see to Naomi's firewood and fetch [me] some clean linen cloths."

Martha gingerly unwrapped her veil from around the bo[y.] Naomi's old eyes widened in horror.

"We will need a large basin of warm water."

Naomi remained statue still. She was unable to hear or und[er]stand anything in those moments.

Martha reached over and touched her shoulder.

"Naomi, the water you are heating for porridge, please, go [get] it. We need to wash him."

Martha's words and touch finally penetrated, and Naomi h[ur]ried out the door.

Then, together the two women spent the first hours of t[he] morning washing the child and tending to his raw wounds.

Slowly Martha was aware of her brother's absence, but wh[en] she questioned Naomi about his whereabouts, Naomi j[ust] shrugged her shoulders and offered, "He left soon after you a[nd] Mary this morning. I watched him go. He went in the directi[on]

the vineyards. I think he wanted to be alone; so I did not
ak or question him."

'I see," Martha said, and then turning her full attention back
he boy, she whispered fiercely, "Whoever had this child tried
id themselves of him by beating him before they threw him at
feet."

Naomi nodded sadly. "Yet, he was not abandoned like so
ny. At least they cared, in some small way, to throw him at a
serby," Naomi reflected.

he morning was almost spent, and the sun was high above
m by the time Martha moved the little bag of human flesh and
es from the cooking area into her room. Tenderly she laid
a on her pallet and marveled that in spite of the bent and
sted legs and the continual oozing of pinkish pus from his
, underneath his borrowed, oversized tunic, a little heart
mped along at a slow, steady pace.

'You are alive, little one, and you will be well!" Martha
ke the words of soothing encouragement over the feverish,
ping child.

a few moments later, as she was on her knees beside the boy
nging his eye dressing, she heard Mary's voice behind her.

'He is alive, Martha!" Mary cried.

Had Martha looked up she might have grasped the full sig-
cance of Mary's statement by the glow on her sister's face,
Martha continued changing the boy's dressing.

'Yes, I know," Martha answered, without looking up.
aomi and I cleaned him, although it was a very difficult task.
w he is still very sick, but he is alive."

'Martha, you didn't hear what I said." Mary shook Martha's
ulder and turned her face upward.

He is alive." Mary's voice was clear and deliberate.

'I heard you, dear sister, and I am just as pleased as you are. I
w the child will live and his wounds will heal. Now, tell me,
e you able to find the tomb alright?" Martha got up and
ered the boy with a linen coverlet.

I mean *Jesus*, Martha. Jesus is alive!"

Martha stopped, dropped the cover, and, turning, looked
ight at Mary and questioned, "Jesus? Jesus is alive?"

"Yes, Jesus. He is not dead. He is alive!"

Martha took three slow, deliberate steps toward Mary, with both hands on her sister's shoulders, she asked with qu urgency, "You are positive of this? You talked with him?"

"Well, no. I didn't speak directly to him, but I am quite su saw him."

As if the wind had suddenly disappeared from a boat's sa Martha's voice was flat with disappointment. She smoothed hair back with both hands and said, "We are both very tire can see how going to the tomb has been a terrible strain on yo should have never insisted on your going . . . ."

Mary shrugged off Martha's explanation and with a sm show of defiance said, "That's just it, my sister. I went to tomb, but he was not there."

"Not there?" Martha gasped, and then blurted out, "W have they done with his body?"

"No! Listen to me," Mary cried, and taking both Marth hands in hers, she said, "Joseph's servant Amon took me to garden, pointed out the path which led to the tomb, and then left. I followed the path, and when I came around some tr past a small bend in the road, the open tomb was in front of m wondered why the entrance stone was way off to the side a down the hill a bit. The whole idea of going into the to frightened me so, Martha. My bones were like melted w within me. But I was determined I would go in. I have ne been so afraid in all my life!"

Impatiently Martha interrupted, "You said he was gone? W the tomb completely empty? Did they move his body to one the niches or perhaps to another tomb?"

"Martha, he was gone, but the tomb was not empty."

A few moments of shocking silence hung between them bef Mary continued. "Two men were sitting very still on the s benches. I jumped with fright when I saw them, but I didn't or leave them. Without my asking, they read my inner thoug because one said, 'He is risen from the dead as he said would.'

"I was so awestruck I don't know if they said anything els

ly know I left the tomb and wandered up the path to a high
ce in the garden.

'I was trying to sort it all out in my head when dimly through
 tree branches and back down the hill a few paces I saw a
man sitting on a garden bench. She was crying and sobbing
o the folds of her skirt. I was going to go to her, because I
membered you said Mary Magdalene or Jesus' mother might
 there. But just then a man approached her, and they talked.''

'Was it Jesus?'' Martha hardly dared to ask.

'His back was to me; so I really don't know except that the
man fell to her knees, and I could see her face as she looked
 at him. It was Mary Magdalene, and her face was a picture of
re joy. Martha, the man *had* to be Jesus.''

'What happened then?'' Martha eagerly questioned.

'Well, it looked like Mary tried to kiss his hands, his feet, or
ybe just the hem of his garment. I'm not sure. But he stepped
ck and said something quietly to her. Then Mary got up and
 down the hill out of my sight.''

'Didn't you go to him?''

'Yes. Immediately I ran down the path, but my skirt caught
 a bramble bush, and by the time I freed it from the thorns and
umed my descent, he was gone. The stone bench was empty.
e path, trees, and flowers were quite still. No one was there.
 I came home.''

'Then you don't *really* know if he is alive or not?'' Martha's
rds were gentle, but firm.

'The man had to be Jesus,'' Mary replied stubbornly. "Bees,'' Mary continued, "all the way back home this morning, I
pt remembering that he has always told us what would hap-
n. Jesus said in so many ways and so many times, that he
uld die.''

'But did he ever say he would raise himself up again?''
artha countered.

'Yes, I think maybe he did.'' Mary's eyes were glittering with
w excitement. "Remember, he said the temple would be de-
oyed, and that in three days it would be raised up?''

Martha nodded somewhat slowly.

"You and I and Lazarus and I'm sure most of the discipl took it for granted that he meant the temple buildings Jerusalem, but what if he meant his *own* body? It's been th days now since his crucifixion. What if he was talking abe himself?"

Oh, that I could wholeheartedly believe all of this, Mar sighed to herself as she ignored Mary's logic and guided her of her room and into the great hall.

Mary's gift of discernment led her to say, "Martha, why you find things so difficult to believe? We have seen Jesus, w our very own eyes, raise Lazarus from the tomb after brother had been dead for four days. If he could do it for sor one else, is it not possible he could do it for himself?"

"Yes, I suppose so," Martha said cautiously. She looked o at her sister. A small golden shaft of sunlight from a lattic window was playing games in Mary's hair, and her face, thou puzzled, was exquisitely beautiful.

You have always found it easier to believe, Martha thought she looked at Mary. *You hug each day as if it were your long-l friend. I cannot do that so readily. I accept the days as th come, but I prefer to keep them an arm's length away whil examine them.*

Martha was about to logically explain her reluctance to lieve when both women were interrupted by the banging noise the front gate. They ran to the door, out into the courtyard, a came face to face with a very agitated Andrew and a wide-eye speechless Lazarus.

Both men were breathless, for they had traveled the last ste hill on a dead run, under the full heat of the midday sun.

"You . . . will not believe what . . . has happened," Andr managed to gasp.

Try me, thought Martha somewhat sarcastically.

"It is true then?" Mary cried before Andrew could catch breath. "He is alive? I knew it. I knew it!" Now she was jun ing up and down and clapping her hands.

"Yes, dear friends, Jesus is alive!" Andrew picked Mary up one effortless move and swung her around the courtyard, lau ing and shouting.

'Andrew," Martha called sharply. "Andrew, have you seen
 with your own eyes? Have you talked with him?" She
ted for his confirmation or denial with both hands on her
s.

ndrew didn't stop his dancing nor did he put Mary down. He
ed over his shoulder, "Mary Magdalene saw and talked to
. Then Peter and John went to the tomb, and it was empty."

Martha shook her head impatiently and shouted, "An empty
b does not mean someone lives. It only means the tomb is
ty!"

ndrew stopped whirling Mary and faced Martha, saying, "I
 you, woman, he is alive. Jesus is alive!"

Martha looked over at Lazarus. "What do you say to all
?" she charged loudly.

azarus's smile was as broad as his face would allow. He
ok his head. "Martha," he said, putting his arm around her
ulder, "Martha, I am the last, the very last person on earth,
oubt Andrew's words. I am living proof that this Jesus, this
 of God, has power to do all things. It is not possible for me
oubt, for I have been rescued and restored. He is alive, dear
er. You wait and see."

h, dear Lord, Martha breathed, *how I wish I could believe it
e true.* Her thoughts pounded along with her heart within

ater that afternoon Andrew left to find and join the other
iples. Martha had no heart to say her farewells; so she was
 Lazarus had spent time at the gate speaking privately to
drew.

he afternoon and evening was a confusing series of events.
ple came and went. Martha divided her time between talking
xcited friends and neighbors, listening to all kinds of wild
ors, and tending the sick, fevered boy.

ven Claudius came. Martha's overly taxed and weary mind
k in his account. But when she questioned him on her impor-
t query, she found he had not actually seen Jesus either. He
 only talked with the soldiers who guarded the tomb.

'I cannot understand it!" Claudius had exclaimed as
ryone crowded around him. "I know all of those men. They

are brave soldiers. They would never shirk their duties. I ha
even fought side by side with two of them in battle. Yet, they s
they 'fell asleep' while on duty, and that when they awoke, t
seal was broken, the stone moved aside, and the body gone
fear they know more than they are willing to divulge. And
strongly suspect someone, perhaps the old foxes of the Sanhe
rin, has sealed their lips with a substantial bribe.''

Martha thought the night and all the incredible things she w
hearing would never end. Finally, she escaped to the silence
the rooftop, and settling down on the wide edge, she ponder
all she had heard that day.

Then slowly, very slowly, even without her really knowing
understanding it—acceptance came. Quietly she said to t
night, ''My Jesus is not dead. He is alive.''

It was a knowledge that did not sweep over her soul w
flashing joy as it had with Mary, Lazarus, and Andrew, but c
that came softly and gradually. The assurance that he was ali
came like an early-morning mist which glides and steals over t
hillsides unnoticed by anyone. Martha didn't see it coming u
the truth of Jesus' resurrection completely covered her.

Then, with only the moon and the stars as her companions
flood of peaceful joy filled her whole being, and before she h
positive proof of his resurrection, she let her relief and happine
mingle with her tears of gratitude.

Between sobs she talked to the night.

''Oh, Lord, I wanted to believe you were alive. I really d
But so many confusing, puzzling things have happened lately
feel we've been living in an upside-down world.

''You know me well, Lord, and nothing has made sense to r
this spring.

''Forgive my doubting, practical heart. You have made n
and you know my limitations.''

Martha remembered the psalmist's words, ''Oh Lord, y
have examined my heart and know everything about me,'' a
she smiled with the comfort they brought. He knows me, s
said, and as she thought about God's forgiving, knowing lov
some of the guilt she felt for having been so reluctant to belie
was eased.

Martha's mind moved from ''He is alive'' to the next issue;

t loud to the sky she asked, "What does it all mean? Where do
e go from here, Lord?"

Only a screech owl answered, but it didn't seem to matter.
artha rose from the roof ledge, dusted off her skirt, and left the
of wearily and with a deep inner gladness warming all the
oms of her soul.

Andrew came the next day. "I must speak to Martha," he said
Mary as he entered the great hall.

"If you are here to convince me that Jesus is alive, you have
me on a useless errand," Martha said cheerfully as she
ossed the floor to greet him. "I know, here," she said, as she
aced her hand above her heart.

Andrew responded with a beaming grin. "Ah, I knew you
ere having a hard time yesterday; so I came back to tell you
at I have seen Jesus." He tapped his eyebrow and continued,
With my own eyes."

"Tell us everything!" Mary begged in a breathless whis-
r.

"Where were you?" Martha's question rang of practicality.

Andrew sat down on the couch and motioned for Martha to sit
side him. Mary plopped down on the floor in front of him, and
azarus pulled a chair closer to them all.

"When I left here yesterday, I went back by the main road.
ilip, James, and John were heading this way to find me; so we
went back to Jerusalem to search for the rest. It was a difficult
sk, because we were not sure what the Jewish leaders would
to us if we were discovered, and none of us had any idea
here the rest of the disciples were.

"Finally, with Joseph of Arimathea's and Nicodemus's help,
eryone was found except for Judas Iscariot and Thomas. I
n't know where Thomas is, but I'm sure he is around. As to
das Iscariot, there are terrible stories and rumors raging about
m. None of us have seen him since the Paschal Supper. We
ar the rumors are true and he is dead.

"We needed a secret place to meet; so we gladly accepted
codemus's offer of a large room. He owns one which is above
me shops in Jerusalem.

"It was while all ten of us were eating a spare and hastily
thered meal that Jesus came."

"Then he looked the same as before the . . . ." Mart
didn't use the word *crucifixion*, but Andrew knew what s
meant.

"Well, yes and no. It was Jesus, and we had no trouble reco
nizing him; yet almost everything was different or changed abo
him."

"Like what, specifically?" Lazarus leaned forward in h
chair as he asked.

"In the first place," Andrew's face showed a hint of a smi
"when we first saw him, he was standing by us in the roo
although he had to come through a locked door to do it."

Lazarus shook his head.

"What did he look like? Had that changed?" Mary asked.

"Yes, he was changed." Andrew lowered his eyes an
studied the carpet beneath his feet. "His wounds were . . . the
were, unmistakably the Master's. He showed them to us; so w
would not fear that he was a spirit and would be able to believ
that it was really him. But it was his face which was the sam
yet different, all at once.

"Even when I first saw him at the Jordan River with John th
Baptist, I was struck by the majesty of his face, but now that h
has accomplished his task, I've seen the truly majestic face of
king."

"What did Jesus say, and what happens now?" Martha
curiosity was getting the best of her.

"Jesus spoke of our preaching the Gospel everywhere
everyone. He said, 'As my Father has sent me, so send I you.

"All of us struggled with the joy, amazement, and incredibili
of the whole night. For we knew what we were seeing and hea
ing; yet it was all so farfetched in the light of everyday events.
least I know one thing, and that is we are all going to Galilee. I'
sure Jesus will tell us much more when we get there."

"Do you think Jesus will come here, to Bethany?" Mary wis
fully asked.

"I cannot say, for I know nothing of his plans."

Andrew looked over at Martha and said quietly, "I must b
leaving now, but I wanted to come back today and tell you
him. I also wanted to say my farewell to you, before I go

*ernaum. Ah, to all of you,'' he added.

Martha dropped her head, so he would not see her disap-
ntment. She stammered, "I . . . I shall miss you. Perhaps
Lord will send you back to work here in Bethany or
salem?'' She asked the last question hopefully.

ndrew reached over and took her right hand in his and said,
Jo not know how or where we disciples will serve the Lord.
do I know when I shall return to this special house. I just
it you to know I feel . . . .'' He did not finish the sentence,
he saw Lazarus's and Mary's eyes open wide with more
stions.

uickly Andrew turned from Martha and said to Lazarus,
e leave now for Galilee, but I shall ask the Lord about your
re, and I'll get word to you somehow.''

With an abrupt and hasty farewell he was gone, and Martha,
ing to Lazarus, asked, "What was that all about?''

Mary quickly interjected, "I think I can guess." Then directly
er brother she said, "You want to be a disciple of Jesus,
't you?'' His answer was an affirmative nod.

I see,'' Martha said aloud to Lazarus, and then, to assure
of her approval, she added, "Blessed be the name of the
d.''

wo Sabbaths passed. Martha and the others heard nothing
:ual nor did they see Jesus or any of his men. Only one rumor
put to rest, but that concerned Judas Iscariot.

t seemed it had indeed been Judas who lurched past Martha
Mary like an angry, drunken man the night of the Paschal
pper. Then after he betrayed Jesus with his salutation of
abbi, Rabbi, hail,'' and his kiss, Judas compounded the evil
hat night by ending his own life viciously and without mercy.
one in the house of Martha could speak openly about it; so
y closed their minds to his name and deeds.

few mornings after the third Sabbath, Martha rose right at
vn to check the restless stirring of the boy Lazarus.

he was pleased with the way his eye wounds were healing,
physically he seemed stronger each day. It was the dark
mories which seemed to plague him at night that she had no
dicine for.

Maybe some warm tea will soothe his troubled mind, thought, and she left him to brew some herbs.

It was barely light outside, but she kindled the fire in courtyard and hung a pot of water above it to heat. Then Mar went back inside and took down her treasured pots of herbs spices from a cupboard shelf. When she felt she had found j the right blend, she placed them in a pottery cup and went c side for the water.

Just outside the doorway, Martha dropped the cup, and fragmented into tiny pieces at the feet of Jesus.

"My Lord!" Martha gasped.

"I'm sorry I frightened you, dear Martha," he smiled, and the fresh new light of day, she could see it really was him immediately her fear left her.

"Here, sit down." Jesus led her to a wooden bench beside servants' quarters, and he sat down beside her.

For a few moments neither of them spoke, and the cool, cl day was still except for a rooster's brave announcement t morning had come.

"Oh, I am glad you are here, Master," Martha fina breathed out.

"Yes, I am, too. This is a beloved place for me," he said, eyes taking in the back courtyard surrounding the brick ove and open cooking fires. Then abruptly he asked, "Tell me, y have found the boy I sent?"

"Ah," said Martha with understanding, "so it *was* you w allowed me to find him. Yes, I have him here. His wounds a afflictions are grievous, but I'm taking care of him. In fact, t was to be a beneficial tea for him." She pointed to the brok cup and smiled.

"Let's go see him."

They moved silently into the house, through the cooking are hall, and into her room. Martha pushed the tapestries back fr the window, and the sunlight warmed the room.

Jesus knelt down beside the sleeping boy and smoothed hair. The boy stirred, opened his good eye, and turned his he to see who touched him.

Softly Jesus talked with the child, but Martha could only he

...ches of words. Her vision blurred with tears when she saw a ... hand come up out of the quilt to touch Jesus' beard.

...hen gently Jesus helped Lazarus to sit up, and the boy's legs ...gled grotesquely over the side of the pallet.

...'ithout getting off his knees, Jesus said to Martha, "I don't ...t you to miss the path I've planned for you, Martha."

...he didn't know precisely what path he meant, but her spirit ... willing; so eagerly she said, "Master, I shall follow any path ...'hich you lead me."

...e turned his head away from her and back to the boy. Then, ...e massaged the boy's legs with both his large hands, he ...d, "Martha, will you feed my lambs, like this little one?"

..."You know I will," she answered, her face wet with tears. ...:sus did not reply. He helped the boy to lie down, and then, ...ering him up, he looked down at the child and said, "Martha, ...uch as these, belongs the Kingdom of God."

...hey walked out of the room, and Martha inquired, "Shall I ...e the others? They will want to see you."

...e shook his head no and whispered, "I will see them and ..., too. Later. Do not call them. In fact, you had better go and ...e the child his tea. He will be needing it."

...artha glanced behind her down the hall to the open door-..., and when she turned back to say her farewell to Jesus, he ... gone! He had vanished as instantly as he had appeared.

...ven Mary will not believe all of this, she thought.

...hen the same improbable song she sang on the day with ...rew—the day she believed—began to stir within her, and ... hummed the melody all the way out to the pot in which the ...:r was merrily bubbling itself away.

...y the time she cleaned up the broken pottery, fixed a new ...d of herbs, poured the hot water into the cup, and let it set ...ile to cool, the sun was fully over the hills. Also her song ... no longer a hum, but a loud, full-blown solo to the morning, ...oleander blossoms, and some very startled birds.

...aomi peeked curiously around the corner, and when Martha ... that her old face was gathered together in a frown, Martha ...ked cheerfully, "Should you be wondering, I am making a ...ul noise unto the Lord."

When Martha entered her room with her cup of hot tea, for second time that morning she dropped the cup and it brok splattering pottery, water, and herbs all over the floor.

The young lad was standing by his pallet looking dowr something he'd never seen before—straight legs. Just below tunic were two regular little knees; below that, two regular li legs; and at the bottom, on the cool stone floor, two regular li feet.

Martha fell on her knees beside him, and holding him cl she buried her head in his shoulder.

Not long after that amazing morning, scores of people Jesus, talked with him, ate with him, and as Martha her witnessed, were utterly awestruck to see him leave.

Aaron and Jude had burst into the house yelling, "Jesu coming here. He is on his way up from the main road." instead of coming to her house, the small crowd of people tur the other way and went up toward the hills.

Martha and her entire household eagerly followed. Then, a a few brief words, Jesus ascended before their very eyes cloud of glory above the green-carpeted hills of Bethany.

He parted from them promising his return. So with one h shading his eyes from the bright glory which surrounded h and waving with the other, each of the small band believers—wondering what it would all lead to—stood gazing into the heavens long after he had gone.

13

E first year after Jesus ascended, the family in the house of
tha and the people of Bethany resumed their lives in a tenta-
way. Always they kept a watchful eye for Jesus, and they
d alertly, ready to leave everything in the event of Christ's
rn.

hey talked of nothing else and reminded each other daily that
s promised to come back and take the believers back
venward with him. A feverish excitement ran through their
s, and they searched the skies continually.

ven Martha was caught up in "Jesus watching." She man-
d to carry on with her household duties and tended to the
y physical needs of the boy, Lazarus, but she had her own
ate theory about Jesus' return. Martha was sure it would be
he Sabbath; so with each Friday's sundown, she went up on
roof to be the first to see him.

You'll see," she had said to Mary, who questioned her as
prepared the grapes ready to become raisins on the drying
s one morning. "Jesus will come back after he has had a few
ks in heaven with the Father. You'll see."

ut as the weeks turned into months, Martha began to have
bts. Then Mary remembered Jesus' story about the fig tree
about its budding blossoms which mean spring is come. So
reasoned that since Jesus followed that story by saying he
ld return, then he must have meant he would come back in
springtime.

owever, by the time buds became blossoms, the sheep were
into their lambing, and the hills had turned their first bright
ant spring green since he had left them, there was still no

sight or sign of him and everyone was forced to move
predictions further into the future.

One Sabbath Simon spoke privately with Lazarus outside
synagogue. Both Martha and Mary waited down the road u
an olive tree, their ears straining with curiosity. Expecta
they watched Lazarus come toward them.

"Simon has remembered something about Jesus' retu
Lazarus explained as they walked the short distance home

"He suggested that since Jesus told us all that no man w
know the hour of his return, perhaps it is not wise or even
to keep setting our hearts upon Jesus' imminent return
spring or even this winter. Simon's exact words were, '
chance it is better to live expectantly, knowing in our hearts
he will come back someday. But in the meantime, we sh
grow into obedient and loving people until he does return.'

"His words do make sense, Lazarus," Mary said. "For J
said to work, for the night is coming, and he also said we wen
occupy until he came back."

So they mutually agreed to stop setting a time for Jesus' re
and to go about the business of living watchful lives, pleasin
God.

From that day forward Martha's favorite bit of rhetoric, w
she quoted often, was "Let us all bloom where we are plante

Martha became so caught up in her daily tasks in Bethany
so desirous of doing God's will that when Andrew sent a r
sage requesting a time alone with her to talk, she jumped,
the speed of a gazelle, to some erroneous conclusions. She
sure Andrew wanted to tell her he was about to settle
Bethany, take a wife (preferably her), and teach others about
risen Messiah in Bethany and perhaps even in Jerusalem's t
ple.

She could hardly contain her gleeful heart!

The week before Andrew's visit, Mary added to Mart
enthusiasm, because she made all sorts of comments about n
ing a special wedding gown for Martha, and even once sugges
that Martha and Andrew have a double wedding with her
Claudius. The sisters stayed up late into the night making ha
plans.

artha found herself pacing the floor the hour before Andrew
ved, and she was slightly dismayed that her demeanor was
ut as calm and mature as that of a flighty young girl.

artha saw him at the gate long before Mary or Lazarus,
ply because she had spent all morning searching the road.

Andrew!" She ran to meet him. He had been to his home in
nsaida for several months.

Shalom, dear Martha," he said, grinning broadly, and he
e her a heartwarming hug.

Ah, I see you have been fishing again," she said, taking both
ands in hers and greeting him in high spirits. "Your face has
n burned by the sun and wind of the Galilean sea." Martha
ted happily as they walked arm in arm through the court-
.

ndrew bid Mary and Lazarus a good morning and heartily
raced them both. Then, seeing that young Lazarus was
y peeking from behind the couch, he called with his eyes
kling, "Surely that boy who hides over there is not the
wny, bony little fish I once saw lying all folded up on his
et like he had just been washed up on the beach—is it? No, of
rse not! Why, that one could not stand, talk, or flap his tail!
w, this boy is different. Come, let me see how strong you
e become!"

most instantaneously a rapport began between them. The
approached shyly around the couch and let Andrew pick
up. He settled down confidently and comfortably on An-
v's broad knee.

Andrew, you have a marvelous way with children," Mary
erved with admiration.

He always has," said Lazarus. "It was Andrew, you re-
ber, who once found the boy with the loaves and fishes for
Master."

artha thought her already full heart would burst with pride,
ng the tiny boy on the big man's lap.

othing will separate us now, Martha thought. *We are so
d for each other.*

was later that night, after they had eaten and laughed to-
er, the boy had gone reluctantly to his pallet, and Mary and

Lazarus had discreetly removed themselves that Andrew
Martha finally were free to talk.

They went up to the rooftop—Martha's feet barely touch
the steps for the buoyancy of her joy.

She would always remember that the night had never bee
indescribably beautiful. It was as if the moon, stars, and f
jasmine-scented wind, beamed and breathed their bless
down on them as they sat on the wide edge of the roof's o
wall.

"Martha," Andrew began, "I have given much thought a
what I should be doing until our Lord returns. It seems to
that one of the most important things I ever did in my life wa
bring men to Jesus. Now, in the year since our Lord has gor
have searched my soul to discover how I may serve him. C
and over it comes to me: I must continue to do as I have d
since I met Jesus—bring others to him."

"Oh, yes," Martha cried. "You are a chosen man, and G
hand is upon you."

"Our Lord told us," Andrew continued, "to go everywh
and proclaim the Good News." Then, with a great deal of he
tion in his voice, he said, "Even to the uttermost parts of
world."

Martha smiled, not really hearing what he meant, and
said, "How wonderful of you to leave your home in Bethsa
The Good-News message is sorely needed here, and Jesus
say Jerusalem first. This is the right place to begin, Andr
right here."

He released her hands, stood up, and walked a few paces f
her. With his back toward her, he said softly, but with gen
authority, "There are some good men who are responsible
Jerusalem, and they will carry on here." He turned and fa
her. "This is not my place, Martha. I feel the Master would I
me go out beyond."

"Beyond what?" Martha asked, as calmly as she could.

"I don't know. Perhaps Cappadocia, Bithynia, Galatia
even Scythia."

"Scythia?" Martha said, harshly pronouncing the name li
was a disease, and her hand flew to her throat. "Andrew, tel

ı are not even thinking of such a place. The Scythians are barous people—no, worse than that! They live in the depths barbarity. They will reject you and our Jesus, and you will ve wasted precious time."

'Martha . . . ." He sat down beside her. "Years ago Philip ne to me about some Greek men who wanted to see Jesus. lip felt, as you, that the Greeks would reject Jesus or that us, because of the way the Greeks lived, would reject them. t I knew here," he said, as he put his fist over his heart, ithout hesitation, that Jesus meant his Gospel for everyone. rgiveness is for every race, every city, and every nation; so I k the Greeks to Jesus. I was right then, and it is right now that ɔ beyond this country and preach the Good News."

Martha was devastated, but she managed to say placidly, "If ı go alone, I fear the work will be too overwhelming. Are you nning to go alone or will you take someone with you?"

'I don't want to go alone," he answered. "In fact, that is at I must speak to you about."

Iope, like a small bird, sang and beat its wings against her ast.

Andrew took a fresh grip of her hands, and looking directly ɔ her eyes, he said, "Both Lazarus and I have been praying as what the Lord would have us do."

'Lazarus?" she cried and pulled back to more fully scrutinize face.

'Yes. We told no one, as we wanted to be sure of the Lord's ı. But the time for a decision has come; so, after many months prayer, I have asked Lazarus to go with me. Since he cannot a disciple, he wants to preach the word of truth."

Martha gasped in unbelief. "You asked Lazarus?" she asked h considerable dismay.

Juickly he answered, "Yes. Right after Jesus left us, Lazarus ł me he felt the burden to preach; so we agreed to pray over ı, and we have, all this time. This afternoon I asked him to ɪ me. He said my invitation was an answered prayer. Besides, ı sure you don't need him here."

t was some time before she found her voice, and as she re-mbered later, she never did say the wisest words.

Andrew searched her face and then asked, "Are you alrigh

"No, I'm not alright." Martha turned her head away fr
him. Her bluntness startled him.

"I am not well. In fact, I fear it's leprosy, which at this
ment is creeping over my bones, and if it is, you had better le
this roof at once!" She bowed low and made a sweeping gest
toward the staircase.

Andrew admonished sternly, "Now, stop that teasing and
serious. It is alright that Lazarus go with me, is it not?"

"Yes, of course it is." Martha was trying to stop the
smarting tears which were stinging her eyes.

He took her hands in his and said softly, "I'm sorry, Mar
but I do not understand why you are so upset."

"Oh, Andrew," she said, freeing her hands from his grip.
turned away from him so he would not see her tears. "It's
that a silly dream of mine has been shattered tonight. I
wrong to even dream it . . . but I thought you . . . we . .
Oh, Andrew, I've been so foolish . . . ."

Then, not because of what she said, but how she said it,
drew suddenly put it all together and understood.

He walked over to her, turned her around, and very ge
kissing the top of her head, he confided, "It was not a s
dream, nor are you a foolish woman. May I tell you a secret

She had no resistance. She nodded.

"I have cherished you since the day you sailed into Beths;
with your Uncle Judah, so long ago. Peter 'helped' you ou
the boat by roughly jerking you to see how you would take i
was his way of testing you. I liked you instantly because
held your head up high, and you did not cry out or complai
said to myself that day, 'There is a girl who is sturdy and
able. Not even a strong wind could push her around or cause
to complain.'

"I have loved you these past years. Why, I even loved
when you spilled barley soup all over me." He laughed
hugged her close to him.

Then, directly into her ear, he whispered seriously, "
taken no wife, for I have never found a woman who could ma
your goodness or your strength of character."

artha challenged, "But you are going away and not with me,
with my brother, Lazarus . . . ." She pulled back and
ed up at him.

aking her by the shoulders, Andrew explained, "Yes, I
d Lazarus to go, but the decision has not been an easy one,
has it been made hastily. As I said, Lazarus and I have spent
y hours in prayer over this.

have prayed and walked the beaches of Galilee many
ts. I have given serious consideration to what the Lord
ld have me do, and I am like a man possessed, Martha.
must go and spread the Gospel, or I will shrivel up and die.
I must go without you, at least for now.

dread taking a wife on a ship which may sail in rough or
narted waters. To expose a wife to heathen people is too
y, and I have thought much about the heavy responsibility
:h settles on a husband. I may not be able to take proper care
wife."

could take care of myself," she said stubbornly.

Oh, I don't doubt that for a moment. But while I am con-
ed I should go, and I am ready to lose my life in a foreign
, if it's required, I am not willing to ask you to risk yours."

ith quiet resignation Martha knew who had won the battle;
he spoke without bitterness, but a trace of sadness could be
rly heard. "When will you and Lazarus leave?"

If we have your blessing, we will leave right after the next
bath."

So it is settled then," Martha said, looking up into the black
et sky. "I will have them for only three more days," she
to the brightest star, "so I had best make the most of it."

o Andrew she said, "You have my blessings—both of
—although it is the very last thing I want to give. If I had my
, I'd keep you here—all safe and snug until our Lord returns.
. . . ."

Martha," Andrew tilted her face toward his, "You are truly
oman of God."

he pulled away and uttered a short, "Ha. Don't give me too
h praise or credit, for it is only a small part of me that
ases you and Lazarus," she retorted somewhat cynically

and with a shrug of her shoulders.

As they left the private intimacy of the rooftop and came de
the stairs, Martha paused, turned, and took a long, loving l
back up at Andrew's face in the lamplight.

It was good she did, for other than precious glances the r
few days and hastily written, rather garbled messages giver
someone in a passing caravan, it was their last real touch
several years.

God graciously favored the work of Andrew and Lazarus v
a special harvest of souls. First in Cappodocia and then, fina
in Scythia.

Martha had to admit that even though the Scythians v
more "barbarous than barbarians," going there had not bee
waste of time as she had once stated.

"Each day a few more believe," Lazarus's latest mess
read. Martha rolled up the precious papyrus scroll and place
on the table for safekeeping before she took it to read to Mar
Jerusalem.

In those years everything seemed to happen so fast, Ma
recalled.

Not many months after Lazarus and Andrew set out, M
and Claudius were joined together in marriage with Rabbi
Isaiah presiding over the traditions of the day.

It was a beautiful wedding, accentuated by the glowing bea
of both the bride and groom; but it was not a wedding of h
spirited people and joyous musicians as Martha's marriag
Benjamin had been. Only a few close friends and neighbors v
invited, and the wedding feast was given in a dignified mar
but with an aura of subdued grace.

Claudius was still a Roman legate—a fact some people
Bethany could not tolerate. Harder still for some of the Jev
believers was Claudius's own belief in Christ.

"We will never accept a Roman as a true believer," som
their neighbors had said scornfully. But Martha, remembe
Andrew and the Greeks, rose loftily above all the talk and sa
Mary's wedding with enthusiasm, both hands, and a ha
heart.

In spite of vocal opposition, the marriage seemed to g

better as the days went on. Claudius and Mary settled in a
ll house on the outskirts of Jerusalem, and its close proxim-
o Bethany gave Martha and Mary many chances to visit
and forth.

was always hardest for Martha to return home to Bethany.
house was empty, and even with Naomi and the servant
and boys, its chambers held only shadows of old memories.

artha began to see clearly the face of loneliness. Its un-
ted presence was clearly defined in her mind, for it stared
kly out at her from the silent rooms and hallways.

ne would have wallowed and drowned in a deep pool of
pity had it not been for a still, small voice she heard one
ning.

artha had left little Lazarus with Naomi and walked down to
place of thinking, in the grove-garden.

ere, amid the feathery, gray green branches of the olive
s, she first heard it.

er heart stopped for a moment, and then with incredible
er it pounded in rapture.

was Jesus' voice. *He has returned,* Martha thought. Laugh-
out loud she said, "And it is not even the Sabbath." She
around expecting to see him directly behind her.

owever, except for a small brown sparrow who cocked his
and studied her cautiously, there was no one around.

heard you, Lord," she called to the garden. "Where are
? Where do you hide?"

ne craned her neck and bent down to search under the low
ging tree branches to see if by chance he was sitting on the
s. But she could find no one.

Martha, the Kingdom of God is here. I told you I'd never
e you. My Spirit is here now, and it is He who speaks."

3ut, I cannot see you, my Lord," she countered.

is voice was as she remembered it—warm, and clear. His
ds were as she remembered also—about a path.

_ook closely to the path you tread, Martha, for I do not want
to lose your way."

_ose my way, Lord?" she questioned him and was mildly
sed to think she would get lost on such familiar ground.

"Lord, I know this garden path so well, I could run it at n
without a torch and never make a misstep or stumble."

"It is not the garden path I speak of," he answered and tl
ignoring her comment completely, he asked, "What are the
sires of your heart?"

"My desires? Let me think . . . ." And then remembe
the face of loneliness and feeling the lump which stretched
throat in a dull ache, she said, "I suppose because of so m
losses and with so many dear ones gone, I would desire
lonely life I lead to end, to have my house filled with pe
again, and to feel in some small way that once more I am nee
by someone. I am alone now, Lord, you know."

It wasn't a laugh, but more like a low chuckle she heard,
then he said pointedly, "Martha, I told you I would never le
you. You are lonely now, but you are not alone.

"If you seek after me with all your soul and with all y
being, and delight yourself in me, I will give you the desire
your heart."

"The desires of my heart? But how can that be? My hous
empty. My soul yearns for them, but they cannot or will
return," Martha cried.

"I shall fill your house with many people, and you will mi
ter unto them, just as you did for me. Remember, Martha,
gave me more than a cup of water or a night's shelter. '
shared your whole house with me, and your generous hospit;
refreshed my soul many times.

"Now I want you to open your house to others and love tl
as I have loved you. Then the desires of your heart, dear cl
will be granted. Don't miss the path I have opened for you.

"Oh, Lord," Martha was almost in a panic, "how will I kı
to whom I should minister or serve? And how will I know
right path?"

He did not answer, and the stillness was broken only by
harsh, shrill cry of a swallow that swooped low over the gard

Martha left the grove-garden and walked, deep in thou
back to her house. She kept asking herself where, or how,
Master would fill her house.

...he didn't wonder for very long, for an incredible thing hap-
...ed.

A few mornings later, Naomi left the courtyard to sweep the
...t and debris off the front steps and came back carrying not
...y her broom but a basket. She lifted the cover in the basket,
...d Martha exclaimed, "There's a baby in there! Whose is it?"

"Ours, I think," Naomi dryly commented.

Martha peered down at the tiny infant boy, and smiling
...adly, she said, "I feel like Pharaoh's daughter finding the
...y Moses in the bulrushes. First there was Lazarus, and now
...s. Am I to care for this one as well?" Martha addressed her
...arks to no one in particular, because Naomi was already
...rying the basket to the kitchen area.

"Yes, you are to care for him and the others," the still, small
...ce within her answered.

...he others? she wondered.

Martha never fully understood exactly how she acquired so
...ny children, or so quickly. But suddenly, from the most un-
...ected corners, they came. Most of them were mysteriously
...osited during the night at her front gate, and soon she
...covered she had no time or strength to ponder her loneliness.
...Within a few weeks her house was filled again, and to
...rtha's slightly jangled nerves, the house rang with babies'
...es and children's noisy merriment.

...)ne night as she checked the sleeping little people, she
...ught, *I know it is a most commonplace practice for most
...vanted babies to be thrown in wells, left in barrels, or aban-
...ed in the streets and alleyways. But these, dear Lord, have
...n rescued. Help me not to fail any of these little ones.*

Martha found it all very difficult to explain to others. No one
...all of Bethany had ever heard of anyone gathering up the
...pless, homeless children and caring for them.

...:ven Rabbi Ben Isaiah asked, "What are you planning to do
...h all these?" He pointed to Lazarus, who clung to the back of
... skirt and to three other children who were in varying degrees
...distress.

...he reached behind her and ruffled Lazarus's hair. "I don't

really know, Rabbi. I guess I will feed them, try to heal th
wounds, and love them in Jesus' name."

Even Hannah discreetly voiced her uneasiness with Marth
newly founded activities by voicing tactfully, "I admire y
courage in housing and feeding these pitiful remnants of hum
ity, but you cannot hope to save all the children of the world w
are diseased or discarded in a basket on your doorstep."

"That is quite true, dear Hannah," Martha answered, "bu
assure you, I have found what I must do, and I will carry or
the best way I can with the little ones he sends me. I am
caring for them out of some high-handed desire to do go
works, but simply out of my love for Jesus."

Hannah's believing heart digested Martha's words, and th
as she pulled a towel around her voluminous middle, she sa
"In that case, I suspect God will crown all your efforts w
success, and if He does, who am I to deter you in any way
think the best way I can show you my loving approval in thi
to begin with the morning baths!"

Picking up twin girls, as if they were small sacks of gra
Hannah marched off toward the cooking area and the wa
basins, leaving a bemused but delighted Martha behind.

After that, a part of each day found Hannah playing gra
mother with the children, her cheeks flushed and shining w
the pleasure of serving again.

"He has truly given me my heart's desires," Martha said
herself one morning as she washed and dressed. "And never
my cup of life been so filled and running over!"

She dried her face and slipped a clean tunic over her head

"Blessed be your name," she whispered to the still, sm
voice within her.

14

THE mornings seemed to rush by faster than a frightened rabbit
~~ing~~ chased by a hungry jackal. On this particular morning
~~M~~artha felt breathless from all the hurried, noisy activities.

She had, along with Naomi and Hannah, bathed three as yet
~~un~~named infants, cleaned and bound up John and Abram's
~~sc~~raped knees, taught little Ruth the basics of loom weaving
~~(wi~~th a lot of mischievous giggling and not much success,
~~M~~artha noted), and between a score of small interruptions tried
~~to~~ hold a semblance of a conversation with her sister, Mary.

They were finally alone, sitting together in Lazarus's old room
~~wh~~en Mary said, "I didn't see little Lazarus this morning.
~~W~~here is he, and what mischief is he about now?"

Mary sat nursing her own infant daughter, Rebecca, and all
~~M~~artha could see of the baby was a tuft of golden red hair which
~~sti~~ck out of the wrapping blanket. It matched her mother's hair
~~ex~~actly and always brought a smile to Martha's lips.

"The boy is fit and well and, oh, Mary, his mind is quick and
~~ea~~ger to learn about everything. In fact, he is so well he drives
~~me~~ to perplexity for wanting to hear about Lazarus, the Master,
~~an~~d the tomb." She laughed and then continued, "I think he said
~~he~~ was going to meet his friends by the old Bethany well this
~~mo~~rning."

Tabitha knocked quietly and stood in the doorway holding a
~~tea~~rful child.

Martha patted her lap and said, "Give her to me."

She settled the girl down and smoothed the child's hair out of
~~he~~r eyes. Then, holding her close, she explained, "This is my
~~litt~~le Ruth. I fear her ears are forever closed. She will probably

never hear the singing of a lark or the laughter of the oth
children."

"So to compensate for her losses you hug her more often th
the others. Right?" Mary smiled kindly as she spoke.

"Ah, you guessed my secret," Martha said.

"Well," continued Mary, as she rocked her baby, "I've se
you work your magic on many children in the past three yea
especially Lazarus. And I know our Lord, the Great Physicia
shares his healing power with you. It won't surprise me if th
child hears someday!"

Martha buried her face in Ruth's neck, blowing air and tickli
her to avoid the compliment.

Mary was not to be stopped, so she said, "Each time I s
little Lazarus and the way he runs, I am amazed. Remember t
first time we saw him?"

"Oh, I shall always remember! You give me too much prai
though. Remember it was Jesus who touched his legs, not I
Martha patted Ruth's legs as she talked.

"May the Master heal your ears," she whispered into Ruth
tiny deaf ear, "but if not, I'll be your ears as I am one
Lazarus's eyes."

Mary finished nursing Rebecca, and as she tied up the laci
on her tunic, she looked at Martha and the child on her lap a
said, "I wouldn't fret about Lazarus's eye, my sister. What
has lost in sight, you have given him twofold in love! He is
whole boy even with his losses."

Long after Martha had walked Mary and the sleeping Rebec
to the gate, later that day, she pondered the wholeness of t
one-eyed boy, and her tears flowed in an easy joy.

"You said, Lord, you would give us an abundant life a
surely you have," she murmured.

Martha was crossing back through the courtyard to the hou
when, out of the corner of her eye, she thought she saw som
thing or someone move behind the trunk of the largest olive tre
When she saw the edge of a bright blue tunic, she easily call
out his name.

"Lazarus, you can come out of hiding now. I am too old f
you to jump out of trees to try to scare me."

hen he did not move she quickly hid behind a large porch
mn to outwait him. But the edge of his tunic stayed firmly in
e.

eling instinctively that something was wrong or that he had
 some mischief, she moved through the bed of bright golden
ers and bent down beside him.

 turned his face away, but not before she saw his tear-
ked cheeks.

Child, you've been crying." He wouldn't look at her or ac-
wledge her presence for a moment, but when he did, his eyes
ned in surprise.

You have been crying, too, Mistress Martha."

small burst of laughter rippled out of her before she had a
ce to catch it.

Yes, I have been crying, but my tears are tears of joy."

e boy studied her.

Sometimes," she said as she picked up the edge of her skirt
wiped his dirty face, "when you are very, very happy, you
ears of joy. This has been a special day, a busy one, but a
 one; a day the Lord made. And I was just tearfully rejoic-
n it.

Now, tell me," she pried, "were you crying happy tears or
ears?"

Neither," he responded simply.

Really? What then?" Martha pushed for an answer.

e saw his chin snap up in a defiant way, and he said, "I
 angry tears."

Oh, my, the worst kind," Martha sympathized. She took his
 and led him to a bench.

 am not a baby, like Rebecca," he said as he sat beside her.

No, you are not a baby like Rebecca. You are six years old."

Yet I do not know why I cried!" he uttered. "I stayed out
 because I was ashamed for you to see me."

azarus picked up several small stones and threw them idly
st the courtyard wall in front of them.

 secret signal passed between them, and Martha joined his
. For five throws apiece neither of them spoke. The boy hit
ter stone in the wall accurately each of the five times, but

even when she squinted her eyes and took careful aim, Ma
missed.

"I'd make a poor David if I were trying to hit Goliath, a
guess I'd never be a good soldier, either," she observed.

"Oh, no, Mistress Martha," his voice was filled with shoc
vehemence. "You'd make the best soldier in all of Judea. Be
than Claudius or any of his men." He sat very still beside
and almost fiercely he added, "If you were a man, they w
make you the commander of the whole garrison, because
are the best!"

Sensing there was a great deal more behind his words,
slipped her arm around him and pulled him close. Softly
asked, "Tell me, Lazarus, what happened in the village toda

She felt his body stiffen with tension, and she knew she
struck home.

He answered in flat, measured-out tones. "Morticia was t
ing about school and how soon he will be old enough to be
apprentice in his father's wood shop. He asked the o
boys what kind of tradesmen they would be, and then he g
me. In front of all the others he laughed, pointed at me,
said . . . ."

"Come now, what did he say?" Martha wanted the tr
Lazarus hesitated only briefly, and then his words spilled
"He said I was a bastard who didn't have a father, so I'd ne
apprentice in anything."

Martha showed no surprise. She just sighed and ruffled
dark curls on his head.

"Now, Lazarus, we have gone through this before. You k
no one controls the circumstances of his birth.

"I've told you before, that is Jehovah's job. Being born
dying are in His hands. We must take both our births and
deaths as the Lord gives."

Lazarus was reticent to speak, but finally he blurted
"That is not what made me cry."

"What, then?" she questioned.

Martha could see it was painful for him, but the truth bega
emerge as he said, "Morticia said other things."

mm hmm, go on,'' Martha prodded.

ell, he told everyone that I would grow up to be a nothing,
have no father and no mother. I told him I did have a
er and that she was the best. Morticia laughed and said, 'Do
nean Martha is your mother?' Before I could say yes, he
ed at me again and said, 'Why, Martha's never even been
ed. She's the midwife who brings other people's babies
he world, but she's never had one herself.' Then he started
nt with the other boys, singing, 'Mar-tha's no moth-er,
ha's no moth-er.' ''

zarus looked up at her, his little face grave with the hurt of
and asked, ''Is what he said true?''

ell, partly,'' Martha nodded her head. ''I've borne no child
own, that's true, but I once was married.''

was cheered up by the news.

y marriage was some time ago—before Morticia was born.
usband was Benjamin. He was killed in an accident, along
ny father, in Jerusalem. But, tell me, Lazarus. When Mor-
said these things, did you just stand there and cry?''

o. First I hit him.''

see,'' she said, suppressing a smile, for she knew Morticia
everal years older and two heads taller than Lazarus.

id you hurt him with your blow?''

zarus hung his head. ''No, I think not too badly, because he
an off down the street singing his silly song.''

rtha hardly knew where to begin with him, but she stood up
alled to Leah. She said, ''Lazarus and I are going for a
We'll be back soon.''

ning to him, she asked, ''Where would you like to go?''

ou know,'' he said, his face brightening considerably.

h, no. Not the tomb again,'' she groaned.

h, yes. Then you can tell me all over again about the day
walked up to the tomb and said, 'Lazarus, come forth.' ''

don't see that I need to. You seem to know the story better
.''

rtha walked in long, measured strides, and Lazarus took
teps to her two, but he kept up and firmly held her hand.

Because he loved her so, he copied everything about the
she walked, and he was careful to hold his head and shoulde
high like hers.

Out of the courtyard and up the road they went.

Before they reached the tomb, Lazarus asked, a
breathlessly, "Mistress Martha, are we in a race with some
or is someone trying to catch us?"

"Ah! Forgive me, my man," Martha said with laughing
"I was deep in thought about Morticia." She slowed her

When they reached the tomb, Martha did not retell the
of Lazarus's resurrection as she had done many times b
Instead, she stood by the stone doorway and said, "My
when you next see Morticia, there are two things you wi
him."

Lazarus knew a command when he heard one, and his
saluted her with his, "Yes, Mistress Martha."

"First, you will apologize to Morticia for your anger a
hitting him."

The child, wise beyond his years, guessed even befor
said it that she would make him go back to say he was so

"I will," he answered, as if he were taking a solemn oa

"Second," Martha continued, her arms folded in front o
"you will also tell Morticia and any other citizen of Bethan
more thing.

"You will say in your loudest voice, and I know you have
for I've heard you shout. You will say, 'My name is Laza
Repeat this after me." She poked a finger into his shoulde

"My name is Lazarus. My mother is Martha. I am one o
prized olive branches. She is not only my mother; she
father, my brother, my sister, and all my kinfolk. No on
take her away from me, for she is mine and she loves me

When he had repeated it several times and achieved the
inflection in his voice, she asked, "Can you remember all th

"Yes, my mother."

His unexpected answer caught Martha completely off g
and she blushed with ridiculous pleasure. How good the
mother sounded when he said it.

There was nothing more to say, for the look of love

sed between them said it all.

lowly they walked down the hill toward home—each
pped in a cloak of peaceful silence.

s they reached the bend in the road, Lazarus suddenly
ped and said, "Mother, who are those men down by our
?"

artha did not have to take a long look. One quick glance at
tall, reddish-haired man and the dark head of the other told
their names, but her voice failed her for joy.

"Who, Mother? Who are they? Are you crying happy or sad
s?" Lazarus pulled on her tunic.

ow she was shaking her head in disbelief, and the tears were
ing even harder.

inally she said, "These are happy tears, my son. The big man
ndrew, and the other . . . ."

"Is our Lazarus?" he shouted.

"Yes!" she laughed. "Now you can stop bothering me and
him to tell you firsthand about that day at the tomb!"

e ran off ahead of her to greet them, and she watched as the
boy flung himself into the open arms of Lazarus.

ndrew turned, and shading his eyes against the orange sun,
ed up the road.

"Greetings to you, my Martha!" he called heartily.

artha's smile was dazzling. She raised her hand, waved, and
just for a moment she stood straight and tall to gaze at the
and precious people down the hill.

h, Lord, she thought. *I still don't know why I came to love
so late, or why it took me so long to find you. Nevertheless, I
find you, and I do love you! My heart is overflowing with the
der of your goodness!*

song swirled and rang inside her. The familiar words of the
mist filled her soul, and quietly, into the evening winds, she
, "Praise the Lord all nations everywhere. Praise him, all
peoples of the earth. For he loves us very dearly, and his
endures. Praise the Lord!"

hen with her sandals gently slapping the dusty cobblestones,
tha hurried down the street to the outstretched arms of
arus and Andrew.